Praise for *Turning Dead*

"An enlightening, deep, real, illusion- .... opening must read if you are seeking your own real-life answers and personal strength. I love that Ms. Boden isn't afraid to delve into the nitty gritty aspects of real living. Written in a down-to-earth, personal style with deep compassion for the human experience and mystery of life, this treasure is a potent guide to practical living. You'll want to devour every line and put it to work in your life right away."

—Colleen Deatsman, author of *The Hollow Bone: A Field Guide to Shamanism* and *Seeing in the Dark: Claim Your Own Shamanic Power Now and in the Coming Age*

"Staci Boden opens a dialogue to Life's eight great teachers through stories that will inspire you and activate your own story. She is a woman who has walked her talk. *Turning Dead Ends into Doorways* comes at a time when all of us are seeking a way out of the chaos. This practical guide can help us embrace our fear of change by letting go and allowing Life's Mystery to reveal the way."

—Jyoti, Spiritual Director of the Center for Sacred Studies, Ambasssador, International Council of Thirteen Indigenous Grandmothers

"Staci Boden is the ideal guide for navigating the unknown. She is the wise friend, the generous teacher, the compassionate soul-sister you've always wished for. In this book, Staci introduces a practice and a path that will help you move from control to trust, no matter what challenges you are facing. If you are seeking a practical spirituality that makes deep wisdom accessible (and applicable) in everyday life, this is the book for you. If you would like to awaken your capacity to experience grace and gratitude—in any circumstance—this is the book for you. Staci has transformed my appreciation for life as it as—while awakening the possibilities for life as it could be."

—Sage Cohen, author of *The Productive Writer* and *Like the Heart, the World*

"To today's anxious, frenzied world, Staci Boden offers a big in-breath. In *Turning Dead Ends into Doorways*, she lays out the path of 'Practical Spirituality.' Rooted in the ups and downs of daily family and work life, the path embraces the Divine by opening compassionately to the unknown within and without. Boden walks her talk, and as we follow her through the challenges and traumas of her life as a wife, mother, friend, doula and healer, we grow along with her. A candid, rare and immensely helpful book, especially for women in transition or crisis."

—Meg Lundstrom, author of *What to do When You Can't Decide*

TURNING DEAD ENDS INTO DOORWAYS

TURNING DEAD ENDS INTO DOORWAYS

How to Grow Through
Whatever Life Throws Your Way

STACI BODEN

Conari Press

First published in 2012 by Conari Press, an imprint of
Red Wheel/Weiser, LLC
With offices at:
665 Third Street, Suite 400
San Francisco, CA 94107
www.redwheelweiser.com

ISBN: 978-1-57324-491-6

Library of Congress Cataloging-in-Publication Data

Boden, Staci.
    Turning dead ends into doorways : how to grow through whatever life
throws your way / Staci Boden.
        p. cm.
    Includes bibliographical references.
    ISBN 978-1-57324-491-6 (alk. paper)
1. Mind and body. 2. Mental healing. I. Title.

    BF151.B63 2012
    158.1—dc23   2012007837

Cover design by Jim Warner
Cover photograph © Orientaly / shutterstock
Interior by Dutton & Sherman
Typeset in Adobe Garamond Pro and Futura Standard

Printed in the United States of America
MAL

10 9 8 7 6 5 4 3 2 1

The paper used in this publication meets the minimum requirements of the American
National Standard for Information Sciences—Permanence of Paper for Printed Library
Materials Z39.48-1992 (R1997).

For all my beloveds with deep gratitude,
especially Alex, Kira, and Noah.

Contents

Introduction

How Practical
Spirituality Found Me

One day when I was about seventeen years old, my father and I were making cheese sandwiches in his San Francisco kitchen when somehow the subject of Mom came up. I can remember standing in front of the refrigerator looking for mayonnaise as Dad sighed and said, "Oh, honey, if only your mom would learn what she needs to learn, her eyes would be healed."

My world tilted.

My parents had come to San Francisco in 1970, a married Jewish couple from New York with a one-year-old baby girl, me. Whether it was that their young marriage was no match for the San Francisco counterculture or that California water sprouted seeds of difference already present inside them, they divorced within a few years.

After the divorce, each of my parents found happiness in their own way. Mom came out as a lesbian and, with her partner, built a family that is still vibrant today. Dad discovered meditation and eventually founded a spiritual community that also continues to thrive. During that time, my mother was diagnosed with retinitis pigmentosa, an eye disease that was supposed to make her blind by the time I turned eight. Rather than receiving the diagnosis as a death knell, Mom took ownership of her health.

"Healed?!" I attacked. "An eye disease she's had her whole life would magically disappear? That's like saying it's a woman's fault if she gets raped." I didn't tell him that two friends of mine had been date-raped in the last year.

Dad sighed, and his voice slowed to an even pace. "It's not a matter of fault, Staci. It's about karma. About bringing things into balance."

"So Mom was a shitty person in a past life? I'm sorry, I just don't buy it. It's victim blaming." I gripped the mayo, but ferocious rage kept me frozen in place.

Dad uncrossed his arms and shifted positions. "Well, that time you prayed for your Mom in that healing service, I think that helped her."

I was immediately transported back to the summer of my fifteenth birthday when my father invited me on a trip to Europe with his spiritual community. "It's not just any trip," he said. "We're going to pray for peace." Outside, I agreed to the terms, but on the inside, my teenage self thought, *Great, I'll shop while they pray.*

I greeted my father's spiritual community in Amsterdam with skepticism. I didn't understand people who wanted to spend, no kidding, fifteen minutes sitting in a car visualizing light spreading through every orifice of the vehicle. I didn't appreciate a conversation with a man whose eyes were closed because he was looking at me through his psychic vision. I certainly didn't respond well to someone rushing toward me saying, "I see you wearing a white robe with a round talisman around your neck; it's from a past life, maybe Native American."

But then things started happening. On the way into Stonehenge, I fell, tore my pants, and bloodied my knee. I suffered teenage angst while Hilda Charlton, my father's spiritual teacher, gathered the group in a circle to hold hands and magnify the healing energy out to the world. Yet later that afternoon, when I went to clean my knee, there was nothing—no blood, no scab—though my pants were still torn.

Days later, while traveling on a private tour bus, I fell asleep and dreamed a whisper, "Change." Just then, something hit my head and woke me up. It was an American silver dollar. The only person who had walked by swore he'd done nothing. Because first, it was unlikely he could get a silver dollar in the middle of England, second, he didn't know about my dream, and third, he was known to be cheap, I believed him.

Toward the end of the trip, we stayed at a church called Briarwood where there was a laying-on-of-hands service. I wanted a healing for my mom so much, I was willing to stretch beyond my culturally Jewish identity to participate.

Mom's impending blindness cast a shadow over my childhood. When Mom and I ventured out in the world together, I needed to be her eyes. At age five, before I could read, it was up to me to match the alphabet letters Mom made with her fingers so we could find the correct bus home. Mom couldn't see the name of the bus from the sidewalk. At eleven, I walked up and down my Noe Valley neighborhood on 24th Street, leading a blindfolded teacher clicking a white cane against the pavement so I'd learn how to guide my mom after she went blind. At fourteen, I visited the LightHouse for the Blind and put on a mask that simulated the entirety of my mother's vision through two pinprick holes. Immediately, a shroud of darkness turned my sole source of light into a piercing glare, as if someone were shining a flashlight directly onto my pupils. The handrail became my lifeboat, cool steel holding the only hopeful point in navigating a step forward.

Later that afternoon, my arms wrapped around my still-clenched stomach, I stared into my mother's golden eyes and whispered, "I can't believe that's what you see." We sobbed into each other's shoulders. That was the only time we ever cried about her eyes together.

So when the opportunity came at Briarwood Church for me to pray for my mother's eyes to heal, even though I didn't know how to pray and I was concerned about the wrath of my Jewish ancestors, I agreed. I sat on the wooden pew next to my father, silently asking

God to help my mother's eyes heal. Gradually, long-held grief that had never found an exit emerged from my heart as a tidal wave of tears. Pleading sobs shook my body into an instinctual rhythm, back and forth, back and forth, while spontaneous words tumbled from my mouth, "Give it to me, God. Please, I'll take it. Give it to me." These words reverberated through me, uniting into a mantra that carried me to the pulpit. As the minister's palms touched my head, a swirling heat encircled my forehead and eyes. Afterward, I ran shaking from the church, opened raw.

Two years later, standing next to Dad in our San Francisco kitchen, remembering Briarwood stopped my righteous indignation short and tightened my throat into a painful ache. "Why? Why do you think that helped her eyes?"

Dad reasoned, "Well, she's never gone blind."

It was my turn to sigh. I closed the refrigerator door. "Look, Dad. I don't know if what I did mattered or not. Mom has done a million things to help herself heal over the years. For me, that's not the point. It was a really powerful experience. And the rest, I just don't know."

This conversation with my father crystallized both my hunger to engage in the mystical world, to believe in a spirituality that mattered, and my fury with how our human need to understand might cage the mystery and perhaps cause unintended harm. In the face of my mother's potential blindness, finding peace would come through embracing the dark inside the unknown.

As I grew up, my spiritual hunger and skepticism became a paradox that fueled questioning. Throughout college, I practiced meditation and visited psychics, reading books by Thich Nhat Hanh and Starhawk. Meanwhile, people around me were dealing with childhood pain, chronic illness, car accidents, and intimate violations, including sexual abuse. I needed a spirituality that facilitated healing without guilt, judgment, or shame. Something to help me face the fear and discomfort in everyday life that also kept me from burying my head in the sand. Most of all, I needed something that didn't locate spirituality or healing as a distant God or outcome but taught me how to sustain myself from inside. The urge to answer the call coming from my tingling hands and to remember healing from within propelled me to seek a spiritual path beyond blame and certainty.

In 1994, my journey began in earnest after I married my college sweetheart, Alex, and quit law school. Within a week of leaving law school, Alex and I moved to Half Moon Bay, California, and wandered into Oneisha Healing Tools, a store offering products and classes to help people develop consciousness. The moment I met Meenakshi Kramvik and discovered that she and the other healing practitioner owner, Maggi Quinlan, were each enrolled in the very two master's programs I was deciding between, my world tilted once again. Only this time, rather than feeling torn asunder, clarity arrived with synchronicity rooting itself as a guiding force in my life.

I spent the next five years studying earth-based spirituality in a healing apprenticeship at Oneisha while earning a master's degree in women's spirituality at the California Institute of Integral Studies in San Francisco. During that time, I birthed two children and realized how conscious pregnancy initiates transformation and surrender. Apprenticing at Oneisha showed me how to support people, follow energy, and create sacred space. Mothering challenged me to find a balance between service and sacrifice. Sustaining a meaningful relationship with Alex taught me how to hold intimate partnership. Daily life had become my spiritual training ground.

In 1997, I began seeing individual clients, focusing on personal development, energy work, and guided visualization. I also continued my studies, beginning four years of training in non-ordinary states of consciousness with Jyoti, Russell Park, and Darlene Hunter in what is now the Center for Sacred Studies. In 2002, I started cofacilitating different groups: I cocreated Sacred Dance, an evening of freestyle, intuitive body movement to realize dance as a spiritual practice; I assisted Maitri Breathwork, a transformative experience developed by Jyoti and Russell Park; and I offered holistic childbirth preparation by cofounding Birthing Intuition, becoming a certified birth doula in the process. Today, I continue to draw strength and practices from my eclectic training, though I'm not connected with any specific line of healing beyond a school within the Center for Sacred Studies and some fantastic mentors.

Over the years, most of my clients arrived with minimal experience in earth-based and women's spirituality. To meet them where they were, I needed to find words and ways to close the gap between Western thought, earth-based teachings, and feminine wisdom. Practical Spirituality became a bridge to help people enter into a relationship with the unknown inside themselves and daily life. Gradually, eight teachers of personal and spiritual exploration have emerged as a way to study Practical Spirituality: fear, awareness, choice, body, intuition, energy, intention, and surrender. These teachers aren't human, but they are dynamic doorways for awakening consciousness. It's through interacting with these teachers in your daily life that you can practice navigating energy and facilitate your own spiritual connection.

1

Entering the Unknown, One Step at a Time

In reaching for this book, some part of you may already be recognizing a need to do something different in your life. Perhaps you've experienced violation in the past and continue to feel surrounded by damaging relationships. You're bored at a job and don't know how to find inspiration. You're aching to feel a baby's chubby thighs grip your hip but haven't conceived, or even met a partner. You're experiencing stomach pain and suspect that you need more than a diagnosis. You're considering divorce. You're committed to growing awareness, but you find New Age spirituality disappointing. You've lost a sense of who you are beyond being a mother. After years of great psychotherapy, you feel stuck and talking is no longer enough.

In all of the above, there's usually a sense that something is off and there's got to be another way. A transition moment regarding relationships, work, finances, parenting, or health is on the horizon. The energy of your own potential is inviting you into the unknown.

If you are someone who gets to pause before making a choice to transform your life, count your blessings. There are many people who don't have such a luxury, who are thrust into the unknown by life's circumstances.

If you are struggling with something like cancer, chronic illness, years of infertility, the sudden loss of a beloved, or financial collapse, you are already immersed in the unknown. Essentially, you're balancing on the razor's edge between survival and extreme jeopardy in an immediately physical, emotional, or perhaps spiritual way. It's true your reality doesn't offer you the same kind of choice as the person who gets to take a big in-breath before deciding to awaken. You know that God laughs when you make plans, you recognize that control is an illusion, and you've been stripped bare. This can feel like a violation, and perhaps you're feeling raw inside this naked truth *all the time.*

For all those facing challenges from health to money to inexplicable loss, my heart is with you. The truth is, the unknown is waking you up by pulling you into the mystery through what's happening in your daily life. I recognize that hot aching fear might be burning a hole in your stomach. I'm so sorry for your pain, and my words mean nothing. I wish I could wave a magic wand and make your life easier, but I can't. I respect that you might need to get really furious. Shout. Cry. Grieve. I realize this may take awhile.

I don't know why life has dealt you these cards, and I'm not going to try to find answers from the past to make sense of it. Does naming your challenge "karma" really help when you get your fifth migraine in two weeks and your four-year-old wants you to get out of bed and play? If it does, I support you. But if it just makes you feel more helpless and hopeless, then I suggest letting go of the need to know why you arrived at this place. Instead, I invite you to learn how to connect with and navigate through the unknown that surrounds you.

From False Positivity to a Healing Journey

In my experience, Western culture connects happiness with successful achievement. In adulthood, we begin to understand that success isn't always possible. Life is filled with ups and downs, unpredictable and sometimes glorious triumphs, and soul-shattering experiences of pain and loss—all reflecting an undeniable element of unknown mystery.

Many of us turn to spirituality for help in riding the highs and lows of existence. Some people find meaning through attending church, temple, or mosque while others don't feel so safe inside organized religion. I'm someone who—despite an affinity for my Jewish culture—isn't at home in a temple but feels deeply connected to spirituality. For me, the definition of *spiritual* does not necessitate a belief in God but does include a hunger for meaning: an urge to connect with something bigger than ourselves, which can happen through art, work, dance, prayer, cooking, conversation, meditation, parenting, hugging trees, or practicing gratitude. While traveling with my father as a teenager, I had a spiritual awakening that initiated over fifteen years of training and practice with individuals, groups, and small businesses. But just after discovering spirituality, I bumped into some beliefs that didn't jibe with my life experience, a feeling that has only been confirmed over the years.

For a long time, I've noticed how some spiritual beliefs equate achieving a certain positive outcome with healing. The idea that individuals can learn a particular lesson and free themselves from tangible illnesses. The notion that inner work plus positive thought is the road to manifesting exact dreams. The view that reality is a reflection of thought and so bad things can be avoided by changing thought. I've observed that in our humanness, we're trying to make some deals with the unknown mystery of life who some call God: I'll be spiritual and get to be in control. I'll be spiritual and get what I want from life. I'll be spiritual and safe from pain and hardship.

I'm not saying these beliefs are wrong or bad, just that I consistently encounter people for whom these beliefs aren't working. People still lose jobs. Cancer appears out of nowhere. Chronic illness doesn't end. Meeting a great partner isn't happening. Women have miscarriages or can't conceive babies. People are engaging in many different wellness modalities—physical, emotional, spiritual—but they aren't receiving the healing they want. And often, because people can't control the outcomes of these situations, they end up feeling like they've done something wrong. Some of these beliefs perpetuate this idea so that people feel victimized by the very sources claiming to help them.

Yet, what's the alternative? Wanting to achieve happiness by fulfilling dreams is a normal human endeavor. I don't want to give that up. Do you? At the same time, trying to manipulate reality with control can create challenges. Because when reality doesn't look the way we want, in our humanness we may just bury our head in the sand. Today people are questioning the price we've paid—literally—for losing sight of reality in the search for happiness. Moving through the world in denial hasn't really helped most people. Climate change, shrinking environmental resources, and failing economies reveal ongoing global unrest. Especially now, when reality around us is uncertain, we need everyone here with eyes wide open, strong and ready to face current challenges. We need to grow another level of self-reliance so we can sustain ourselves no matter what.

Beyond Control to a Meaningful Unknown

In my healing practice, I offer a different kind of spirituality. A spirituality that moves underneath positive or negative circumstances to help individuals develop internal resources they can access any time. A spirituality that applauds fiery questioning. A spirituality that cultivates personal truth to grow authenticity. A spirituality that accepts pain alongside joy as an equally important—though not equally comfortable—way of finding balance. A spirituality that forgives mistakes in order to learn. A spirituality that shows people how to trust and have faith even when what they think, believe, or sometimes experience makes no sense. Ultimately, facilitating exploration becomes a doorway for people to awaken consciousness and discover their own spiritual connection.

Developing an authentic spiritual connection begins with letting go of using spirituality to feel safe by maintaining control. This doesn't mean giving up traditions that are meaningful to you. Rather, I'm inviting you to loosen your attachment to practicing spirituality as a way to achieve a certain outcome. The key word here is *loosen.* Letting go does not have to mean giving up choice or relinquishing goals. But holding on to a desired outcome with a death grip leaves little room to connect with the unknown mystery of life.

Our desire for control rests on a human need to feel secure and to affirm life. The reality is that control is an illusion. Despite iPhones and Google Calendars, there's no way to truly predict what's around the next corner. We may or may not know small things, like what's happening tonight, or big things, like if we will meet a soul mate, survive cancer, or get pregnant. Nobody knows the exact minute of death. Even if the road taken is familiar, something unexpected can always happen. The unknown is a tangible force that permeates daily life.

Not knowing can feel uncomfortable and can lead to many machinations to avoid facing the truth of what it means to really not know. Instead of relying on control and denial to resist feeling vulnerable (and scared) in facing the unknown, you're invited to develop a conscious relationship with the unknown through daily life. From there, letting go becomes a practice of navigating life in partnership with the unknown to generate meaning.

Spirituality as a Way of Life

Drawing from life experience, spiritual teachers, earth-based training, women's spirituality, and fifteen years as an energy practitioner, I connect the practical with the spiritual to help people find a point of balance between reality and the unknown mystery. Practical Spirituality holds that healing is a journey as much as a destination. If you can let go of control—which is really an illusion, after all—and engage in a conscious relationship with the unknown in daily life, along the way you'll cultivate healing no matter what reality appears on the doorstep.

Furthermore, when you take a leap of faith, the unknown does not leave you stranded and alone but instead responds in the context of daily life with synchronistic events that expand learning. On this journey of meaning, daily life becomes the training ground to transform. Sometimes loss and disappointment happens; sometimes dreams materialize. In the process, you grow your own healing gifts—authenticity, inner authority, trust, faith, peace, gratitude—that have the power to sustain you anywhere because they aren't based on achievement; they're rooted inside.

Instead of perceiving the unknown reality as a big hairy monster in the closet inspiring fear, denial, and blame, you can reframe not knowing into something powerful and also beautiful. You can approach the unknown carefully, even strategically, with respect while embracing its vast and infinite potential. You can learn how to not only trust the unknown but also have fun while growing a relationship there. Along the way to making friends with the unknown, you can take a developmental leap that redefines healing from a positive result to a source of balance practiced in the context of daily life. By entering into a relationship, you give up control but learn how to navigate the unknown.

Your journey begins with choosing one area of life to focus on throughout this book. As you move through each chapter with this focus in mind, eight teachers—fear, awareness, choice, body, intuition, energy, intention, and surrender—facilitate your relationship with the unknown. Each chapter also contains questions, practices, and stories to further your learning and help you indentify your unique healing gifts. To illustrate how synchronicity—meaningful events—informs a relationship with the unknown, I invite each teacher to guide and inform me through daily life happenings. I chronicle my experience throughout the book. In this way, I am with you in navigating the unknown.

Turning Dead Ends into Doorways

Choosing Your Inner Theme or Daily Life Focus

In order to avoid becoming lost in the unknown, you'll focus on one area as you move through the eight chapter teachers. Usually, there's at least one part of life that seems especially challenging. It can look like something negative or positive.

To identify a focus, contemplate unresolved issues in your life. You're looking for what feels most challenging because either you're not getting what you want or you may be about to get it all. You might also consider what you're really attached to. Ask yourself: What would I most like to control? Finally, fears around a life issue can be a helpful indicator of unfinished business.

Some daily life areas include:

- **Body:** health, body image, sexuality, fertility, pregnancy and childbirth

- **Relationships:** life partnership or marriage, friendship, parenting, siblings

- **Career:** vision, work-life balance, productivity, commitment

- **Finances:** self-sustainability, prosperity

- **Creativity:** inspiration, flow, experience, expression (art, dance, voice, writing, music, crafts)

If emphasizing one area of life doesn't resonate, you can focus on a life theme. Usually, this is an overarching pattern that expresses itself throughout your life. For example, I spoke with a woman today who is considering focusing on fertility, not the physical, getting-pregnant fertility but how to awaken potential. If you're experiencing a transitional moment, a life theme may be regarding a particular aspect of development. A sixty-one-year-old woman will focus on herself as an emerging sage to help her embody her next stage of life. Other options could include letting go of a dream or shifting fear to discover your life's purpose.

Whether you focus on a specific outer issue in daily life or an underlying inner theme is your decision. As you grow a conscious relationship, the unknown will eventually inform all areas of your life. My teacher Jyoti has always said, "Inside, outside, same side."

Throughout the book, I'll include exercises to help guide your thought process as you acclimate to working with these new teachers. You may want to take notes about these exercises in a journal or computer document so you can look back later and see your growth.

EXERCISE: Contemplate what you hope to learn through this book. If you are facing a transitional moment, what qualities might help you transform? What could give you strength today?

Intention 101

Once you've identified a daily life issue, pattern, or developmental focus to help guide you through the unknown, the next step is to turn it into an intention. Because intention is a central teacher in this book, we'll study it in depth later. For now, we can start with a few basics. I see an intention as something—usually a word or sentence—that helps you locate where you are in relation to where you'd like to be.

How is an intention different than an affirmation? The language can look similar but the main difference lies in how one holds an intention. I see affirmations as more outcome based ("I am abundant," "My migraines are healed," "I am powerful."). An intention helps you hold the present moment, the unknown, and a possible future.

As I write this, a dear friend of mine is waiting for pathology results after removing a cancerous tumor. Shira Shaiman is the mother of two young boys, a three-year-old and a ten-week-old. In the twenty years I've known her, she's been vigilant about physical, emotional, and spiritual self-care, exemplifying conscious living. She even cowrote a book on nutrition. If Shira can get cancer, anyone can. We're all holding an intention that her pathology results will come back clear. When we spoke recently, Shira named cancer as a journey through the unknown. She considers cancer to be an opportunity to embody her fullest self. So while Shira's holding an intention to be cancer-free, she's deeply awake in the present moment and the reality of the unknown.

Though Shira is an inspiration, there's nothing noble about how she's holding cancer. She told me, "I feel like I'm walking on a tightrope. I need to be smart here." Damn right. It does Shira no good to hang on to a cancer-free ending for dear life, even though it would be understandable. The high stakes require skillful navigation through the unknown. Now more than ever, Shira needs strong inner authority to guide her through this experience. She also needs help.

By maintaining a vise-grip on what a happy reality looks like, we create a narrow margin for response. When the pieces fall into place, hallelujah, life is beautiful. But what happens if reality doesn't match our picture? Myopic vision can take out our eyes—crush us with despair or blind us with denial—and create victimhood in the process. As a practical woman, I'd rather widen my scope of perception to respond to reality with eyes open. As a mystical woman, I've learned that widening my scope involves loosening and letting go of a specific hold on reality. When I do, the unknown often opens a door of possibility in the context of daily life.

Working with an intention is similar to approaching guided visualization. In guided visualization, you enter an inner world that can come alive to begin a conversation of meaning inside yourself. An intention can take on a life of its own too, except the conversation isn't happening just inside. An intention is a conversation between you on the inside and daily life on the outside. Imagine yourself holding an intention (I'm growing strong). That's your half of the conversation. Now see that intention going out into your daily life. What happens in your daily life is the other half of the conversation. Got it?

When you first meet someone, how do you generate a conversation? Do you dominate the interaction by talking at someone? Or do you invite a conversation by also listening? Working with an intention requires an exchange between your inner (I'm growing strong) and outer (everyday events) world. Taking up all the airspace with your vision of reality is not a conversation. It's a lecture. If you would like to have a conversation that leads to a relationship with the unknown in daily life, you need to do more than listen. You need to be willing to shift and change in response to the unknown.

Maybe now you can understand why intention receives a full chapter later in this book, toward the deeper end of the unknown. But just because intention is powerful doesn't mean you can't get your feet wet now. In fact, one reason to choose a focus throughout the book is so that by the time you get to the chapter on intention, you'll be well on your way to swimming laps (shhhh, don't tell).

Your Intention

I don't have a prescription for how to craft an intention. This is about finding *your* way, not mine. But I can offer some hints. Consider the daily life or inner focus you identified in the earlier section. From there, I recommend starting with a one-word intention, which is potent and easier to remember than a sentence. If you feel strongly about a sentence, keep your language open and flexible. Consider a sentence or question that invites a conversation; avoid demanding or lecturing.

Some intentions arrive clearly while others take time to grow. Once you've identified a couple options, try each one on for a while. Notice how it feels inside. The right intention seems to click into place. Because an intention is ultimately a point of stretching, comfort isn't a measure of accuracy. In fact, waves of emotions that surface, like fear, are a sure sign to stay with it for a while. Do *not* get hung up on perfect phrasing. This is about you calling upon the energy of something. If in doubt, start with one word.

Once the intention seems to settle, start interacting with it. Try imagining your intention sitting in different places in your body like your heart or stomach or solar plexus. Ask your intention where it wants to live. Hold it with awareness. See if you can notice how your intention may be trying to guide you. Become a spiritual detective. Explore, play, and invite magic.

SAMPLE INTENTIONS

HEALTH, DISEASE, OR, CHRONIC ILLNESS: Strength. Healing journey. I invite healing tools into my daily life. Empowerment. Health. Release. Growing choice. Please help me grow amazing healing. Patience. Grace. My intention is to make friends with my body. I'm open to receiving. Regeneration. Creativity. Response-ability. Healing medicine. Compassion.

WORK LIFE OR CAREER: Worthiness. Please show me the work I'm meant to do. Realizing potential. Please help me grow work. Vision. Help me release any blocks to actualizing my career. Soul work. Inspiration. Flourishing career. Creativity. Connectedness. Actualization. Abundance. Flow. Help me identify and embody my career. Cultivate. Thrive. Inner authority.

INNER THEMES: Peacefulness. Fertility. Integration. Intuition. My intention is to develop intuition. Purification. Surrender. Transformation. Gratitude. Please help me grow trust. My intention is to fully inhabit myself. Unconditional love. Help me release any blocks for healing. I'm studying how to receive. Receptivity. Opening. Balance. Courage. Trust. Grace. Wholeness.

Once "Carla," a participant, announced in a group, "My body grows tumors. So far they haven't been cancerous tumors, but my body still grows them. I know I need to learn how to work with my own energy so I can stop growing tumors."

I responded, "Carla, I hear that living in a body that grows tumors is scary. If you're called to work with your own energy, I say, right on. If you decide to focus on an intention to stop the tumors, I'm with you. And while you're holding that intention, I encourage you to notice how your intention is already teaching you in this moment. Healing may be stopping the tumors, *and* healing may be growing another level of relationship with your energy body right this minute. But I can't sit here and tell you that if you do all that, your body will stop growing tumors. I hope. I pray. And I just don't know."

I can't promise you that you'll end up pain free or rich or able to have a baby from engaging with Practical Spirituality, but I do believe we can all learn to cultivate choice in some way. Your ability to choose may exist within the real limitations of daily life. Choice may come through *how* you take care of yourself in the face of a challenge—responding as opposed to reacting. In this way, you can hold a simultaneous intention for a specific healing while keeping an eye open to see other ways that healing is already unfolding in your daily life. Ultimately, you can choose to shift your perception in how you engage healing.

Please know you are my heroes.

ENTERING THE UNKNOWN GUIDELINES, YOUR INTEGRATIVE QUESTIONS

- Remember times in your life when you chose to make a change and when you felt thrust into a new unknown through life's circumstances. What are some of the differences? Where are you now?

- What meaning are you hungry for in your life? What kind of spirituality do you need?

- What's your book intention?

2

Signs and Guideposts: Mapping the Unknown through Practical Spirituality

In the midst of embracing the unknown as a source of spiritual meaning, a commitment to keeping it real is important. Otherwise, spirituality can be an act of escapism that blocks clear perception and reinforces denial. The mystical world can be a wonderful wild ride, but it's necessary to balance meaning with purpose or you could risk getting lost in expansion.

Perhaps it's my culturally Jewish skeptical genes or my feministic questioning ways, but a spirituality that doesn't help me interact with my two teenage children screaming at each other is a hobby, not a way of life. Feeling God's breath course through me until I become peace is beautiful. And if I can't embody that peace while negotiating traffic, then I'm truly stuck.

The practical realm provides insight into how to integrate meaning into daily life. Practicality grounds the potential swirly vastness of spirituality and the fear of not knowing to the here and now. It provides a constant balancing point against a potentially consuming experience. Practicality lives in the present moment, a profound guide to accessing, embracing, and navigating a relationship with the unknown. With practicality often come humility and a sense of humor. Anyone who has ever changed a diaper or picked up after a dog can thank the practical for keeping life real.

Practicality helps us walk our talk. How does awareness relate to deciding what to eat for lunch? Where is compassion while arguing with a friend? How are vision and trust part of searching for a new job? By challenging validity and testing verifiability, practicality offers a reflection on the progress made between balancing spirit and matter. This doesn't mean creating carbon copies of experience. Compassion for a friend caught in a lie may look different than a beloved revealing an honest mistake. Because practicality is no fool, it is a great teacher and ally for spirituality.

To encourage gentle learning, this chapter is going to serve as an in-breath before moving forward by introducing teachers, signs, and guideposts to help map the unknown a bit. Along these lines, I'll share some guidelines, tools, and practices that we'll be building upon in each chapter and are applicable in daily life. Finally, I'll introduce you to Practical Spirituality's best friend, synchronicity, and we'll be on our way.

Eight Teachers to Bridge a Conscious Unknowing

I've already mentioned eight teachers that will help guide your journey through the unknown. Interacting with these teachers will help you develop an inner compass for navigating the unknown within yourself and daily life. Each teacher has its own chapter and creates the body of this book:

- Fear

- Awareness

- Choice

- Body

- Intuition

- Energy

- Intention

- Surrender

While these teachers are obviously not people, they're bridges into realms of wisdom that can feel alive. These teachers build on each other. Studying how fear, awareness, choice, and body permeate your life from inside and out provides a foundation for exploring intuition, energy, intention, and surrender. Learning some basic skills will help you stay afloat when you begin to swim in the deep end of the unknown. At the same time, while these eight teachers offer distinct lessons, they unite in wholeness as consciousness. Fear often expresses itself in the body, which is also a great place to become aware of intuition and energy. See how they all connect? Through you.

What this means is that by the time you arrive at the threshold of a specific teacher chapter, most likely you've already met. This is a good thing, because frankly, becoming conscious is challenging enough. If you realize that you've already been practicing the art of noticing when you officially read about it in the chapter on awareness, I say, right on and let's celebrate. Relationship takes time to grow.

EXERCISE: Meet the eight teachers: fear, awareness, choice, body, intuition, energy, intention, and surrender. Which ones jump out at you?

Practical Spirituality as (R)evolutionary Self-Help

The heart of your learning rests inside the relationship you grow through the eight teachers of fear, awareness, choice, body, intuition, energy, intention, and surrender. Normally, when I'm sitting with clients and groups, I don't present these teachers in a particular order. Instead, I listen to hear (intuitively) which of the eight teachers will be most helpful. The challenge here is to breathe life, your life, into these pages so you can practice navigation. So, I'm going to write this book as a journey into the unknown. On my end, I will explore the eight teachers, chapter by chapter, letting go of everything I think I know. I'll draw upon my relationship with each teacher and Practical Spirituality to gather stories and information from daily life to share with you.

I can't do this alone. My intention here is to support your empowerment, to get behind your life learning. Ultimately, my role is to support you in finding your own truth, not ask that you take on mine. I need you to meet me in the unknown in your own way. You can do that by remembering your intention while reading, reflecting, and applying what resonates with your daily life (imagine that we're traveling together and see what happens!). To help you sort through learning, I'm going to offer questions and practices throughout each chapter. I encourage you to pay attention because as you truly enter the unknown, synchronicity—meaningful events—will start happening in your daily life in amazing ways.

So often, we lose sight of reality by getting stuck in hope and expectation. I'm inviting you to loosen your grip on what constitutes a good outcome. It's possible to simultaneously hold focus for an outcome and value the present moment while recognizing that you can't know anything for sure. This is such an important point that I'm going to emphasize it in another way. Practical Spirituality helps people let go of a dualistic either/or reality in order to enter an *And* world by simultaneously:

1. Living in the present moment *and*

2. Holding focus for an outcome *and*

3. Staying in the unknown regarding outcome

Living in the present moment is especially difficult because it's a part of normal development for our minds to get ahead of things to achieve a want. One day years ago, when my son was three, he asked for a banana. As I explained that we didn't have any bananas in the house, his face purpled with rage. Exasperated, I said, "Honey, the bananas are at the store. I can't just make them appear." He stopped and frowned, honestly perplexed, "And why not?! I want a banana *now.*" I don't mean to simplify fulfilling heartfelt dreams into getting bananas, but I do invite you to pay attention to that feeling of "I want." If there's a purple-faced three-year-old inside, you might see what happens if you wait a bit before taking action on the desire. And while you're there, notice if there's a particular fear or feeling underneath your inner three-year-old's desire.

As an example of getting ahead of things here in this book, perhaps one or more of the teachers draws your attention, tempting you to skip to a specific chapter. I encourage you to notice how you feel without doing anything about it. Noticing without taking action, something I invite you to practice consistently, is a first step in learning how to grow a conscious relationship with the unknown. If I had to pick one thing for you to learn from Practical Spirituality, it would be that you discover how to consciously notice, hold, sit with, and follow the energy of something. Okay, so I'm cheating—four steps but one process.

Ultimately, practicing consciously navigating the unknown teaches you how to create an *And* way of life. Additionally, the journey of discovering your own sense of balance between the present, future, and unknown by noticing, holding, sitting with, and following energy is what grows your power. Not my power, not the neighbor's power, your unique power. The beauty of this practice is that how you explore, nourish, and express your power is authentic in nature. The magic of this practice is how everyday moments surprise you with life lessons strangely designed to facilitate just what you need to learn. Daily life becomes the training ground for developing your own power and sense of balance. Rather than guaranteed endings, moving through life this way produces intangible and priceless healing gifts—compassion, creativity, humility, balance, and trust. These gifts unite to form a foundation of resources that grow you into the next expression of who you are, whatever that is.

Practical Spirituality as Sacred Everyday Living

The more you can learn to notice, hold, and sit with an issue, question, or feeling inside with awareness, the more you grow its potential for transformation. In my world, we call this holding space for someone or something in a sacred way. What's sacred, holy, or divine may look different to each of us. Some people consider objects to be sacred. Land can certainly be sacred. My husband, Alex, considers our beloved dog, Roxie, to be sacred. For me, conscious relationship with anyone or anything is sacred. So *sacred* is an intentional relationship that creates meaning in both tangible and intangible ways. Mind you, sacred isn't necessarily easy. Changing a dirty diaper, cleaning the toilet, or picking up after your dog with conscious awareness may test your boundaries of sacred practice.

For Practical Spirituality, growing conscious relationship with the unknown happens through personal development and in the context of daily life. Remember Jyoti's inside, outside, same side. To cover all bases, I encourage you to invite the sacred into everyday living internally and externally.

Following Energy through Practical Spirituality

Practical Spirituality teaches people how to follow the unknown through everyday life. One of my mentors, Jennifer Sugarwoman, calls this "following organic process." I see it arising from both earth-based and women's spirituality perspectives. The intention is to stay in the not knowing until you get to know—which usually only happens for an instant and then you move on to the next level of not knowing (I know, right?). It's by following energy that life becomes filled with meaningful discovery.

This earth-based feminine wisdom runs counter to what our mainstream culture advocates through control. In attempting control, we've actually been taught to get ahead of the very life force—the unknown in daily life—that holds potent lessons for self-realization. In my world, we call this "getting in front of the energy." Here, *energy* refers to the unknown. You can't think your way through the unknown. Learning how to follow and navigate the unknown happens through practice.

One way to practice following and navigating energy is to remember your intention and see what shows up. Conscious living is a practice unto itself. Another way involves cultivating inward practices like meditation or guided visualization. And finally, holding your intention as you move through this book and grow a relationship with each teacher provides foundational practice in following and navigating energy. As we begin that journey, there are a few basic guidelines and tools to remember.

Creating Sacred Space

In order to develop consciousness within, it's important to create some sacred space in your home. This is a dedicated area in your home that becomes a place to learn and grow. Locating yourself physically helps you expand energetically. Creating sacred space is also a physical form of protection, a kind of intentional container. It doesn't have to be big. When I graduated college, my sacred space was a closet. For many years with two little children, my sacred space was a windowsill high off the ground.

The size doesn't matter, but if possible, find somewhere you can sit comfortably in private, even if it's just for a few minutes at a time.

No need to buy expensive items or obtain voodoo dolls to decorate unless this feels good to you. You probably already have items in your home you can gather—a colorful old scarf, pictures of beloveds, shells or rocks found during a walk with a friend, or a small piece of art. Also, ideally there'd be some form of light to be used during contemplative moments, preferably a white pillar candle. Some people enjoy incense, essential oils, or dried herbs like sage or cedar. You might also incorporate music, a journal, and drawing materials into your sacred space. Let your imagination roam free as creativity fosters intuition. An old futon cover with burgundy, purple, and golden leaves transformed my post-college closet into a soft, cave-like haven. How does your sacred space wish to grow?

As part of establishing sacredness, it's important to address the issue of energetic protection. A commitment to developing consciousness through spirituality means opening to the mystery. Here, learning about protection is not a woo-woo concept but a practical necessity. While I'm not saying that ghosts and gremlins are waiting to get you, many traditions believe that the invisible world is real. Being respectfully cautious when it comes to the unknown is practical and responsible. When you meet someone for the first time, do you hand over the keys to your home? In connecting with the unknown mystery, protection helps sort what comes through the door. Though life offers no guarantees, a keen eye and a good lock can go a long way in maintaining safety.

Fostering protection is an intricate study. Protection can be a lit candle or an intentional piece of jewelry. Certainly, creating sacred space in your home enhances security. Protection can also look like calling upon your own invisible sacred support by imagining a circle of love around you or inviting a sacred force to help you. In this chapter, I'll provide basic energetic protection guidelines for gentle engagement with the unknown. But because I'm not living your life, and we're in the unknown here, please remember to be the ultimate authority of your own experience.

Grounding 101

Learning how to ground is a basic form of protection. As an energy practitioner, grounding keeps me from falling over when a client has a big release. As a mother who just welcomed six teenage girls into the house to get ready for a school dance, grounding reminds me to breathe, order pizza, and take nothing personally. While grounding may sound very Californian crazy to you, my friends who know electronics nod their heads in agreement when I explain it.

Electrical wires, like those connected to an electric generator or a utility pole, are considered dangerous when left unsecured. If, for some reason, an energy surge happens and produces a higher voltage, the surge can overload a live wire with dangerous electrical shocks, power outages, or even a fire. So electricians literally ground the live wire by connecting it to the Earth's soil. Grounding wires works because Earth's electrical system is big enough to absorb energy surges. Grounded wires don't overload as easily.

While I'm no scientist, as an energy worker I've learned that human bodies have electrical systems with natural live wiring capable of receiving and transmitting shocks, power outages, or an internal fire. By using your imagination to connect with the Earth, you're tapping in to a resource that can help absorb shock. Whether you have experience with energy work or you're just starting to contemplate energy, participating in Practical Spirituality will turn up the volume in your electrical system so you become a live wire. Learning to ground is practical.

EXERCISE: See yourself as a live wire moving through your life. Are there moments when you feel more "alive" than others? When?

How can you learn to ground? First, please know that grounding isn't about finding the right way—it's about developing *your* right way (is this beginning to sound familiar?). Grounding can take different forms. Imagination helps some people, while others need more tangible methods. To provide a basic foundation, we'll practice grounding in this chapter. Taking a moment to ground before entering any new unknown is an important practice.

Because learning how to ground isn't about following a prescribed method, try on new ideas (play!) to see what works best. A client of mine imagines a hole in a maple tree. Another client breathes down a cord into the earth. I love shaking my hips to ground through dancing. You might also imagine lying on a warm bed of sand. Your ability to ground is only limited by a willingness to let yourself roam. Explore. Have fun. Ultimately, if what you discover helps you feel calm in the presence of six amped teenage girls, does is it really matter if grounding seems silly? Besides, this is your sacred private work; no one ever needs to know.

Over time, you can develop your own grounding methods that last a few seconds or an hour. Grounding is a practice unto itself, and it also provides the foundation for further spiritual exploration. On-the-go grounding is helpful when you might only have a moment to find balance between heavy traffic, aggravated people, or cranky children. Then, I suggest starting with a deep breath. When creating a more contemplative time, ground and then add visualization, journaling, dancing, crying, or whatever might help you learn more about yourself in the moment.

PRACTICE: GROUND YOURSELF

Begin by sitting comfortably somewhere. Preferably, you've created a dedicated spot in your home, even if it's just a small corner, for personal and spiritual exploration. Do something to purify your space—imagine a cool breeze, burn a dried herb like sage, or spray an essential oil in the air. If you have a candle, light it. Imagine something meaningful or sacred enfolding you in a blanket (or a circle; follow your own imagery) of love.

Take three deep breaths into your heart until it feels like a soft pillow welcoming you home. Pay attention to any images, thoughts, or sensations that appear as you settle into your heart. You don't have to do anything with these images—just notice them.

Bring your attention down to your belly. Once again, take three deep breaths until you feel settled, noticing any images or feelings. Just notice. Next, bring your attention down to the base of your spine, where your bottom touches the floor (your sacrum). Take several deep breaths until you feel relaxed, once again noticing anything that appears as you breathe. Imagine that each breath opens the base of your spine.

As your sacrum opens, see a cord—it could look like a root, a rope, or even a beam of light. See it sinking down, down through your home, through cement, down into dark, rich soil; see your cord moving through rock and water and soil until it reaches molten rock. Allow your cord to sink into that molten rock so that it touches the center of the Earth.

Keep your attention on your cord, that rope or root or beam of light— however your cord presents itself to you—and breathe up the earth energy, through the molten rock, the rocks, the soil, the water, until you breathe up earth all the way into the base of your spine. You may experience tingles, heat, colors, or love. Just notice. From there, keep breathing and imagining this earth energy spreading throughout your pelvis, down the front and back of your toes, up your legs, back, and stomach to breathe earth straight into your heart.

Allow your heart to radiate earth energy throughout the rest of your body, out to your fingertips and up to your head. Imagine the top of your head, your crown, can open and then breathe out any excess earth energy. You may see it as a waterfall or a beam of light. Allow the earth energy to appear any way it wants. You can take a moment to ask that waterfall to be as thick or thin as you need to create protection.

Next, breathe into your heart once again. Extend your awareness up from your heart and out the top of your head past the Earth's atmosphere, and connect with a star. Breathe in star energy through the top of your head and into your heart. Feel that star energy connect with your whole body. Ask your body to find a perfect balance of earth and sky—your body knows just what that feels like inside. Notice any colors, sensations, images, or words. Offer something back to the earth and stars for what you've been given. Take some deep breaths, noticing how you feel. If you want to take a moment to remember this experience, you can. Open your eyes when you feel complete. Remember to say thank you to your blanket of love, take it off, or not, and blow out your candle in your sacred space.

A free audio downloadable version of this grounding is available at *www.dancing-tree.com/book.*

Guided Visualization Develops Key Insight

Once you feel safe and grounded, you can enter your inner world through accessing imagery. There are many ways practitioners invoke the power of imagery with clients. A growing body of data reveals how guided imagery and even hypnosis can manage stress, enhance job performance, and increase health. I'm not so interested in guided imagery that focuses entirely on manifesting desired outcomes, though I'm not saying it doesn't work for some people.

Instead, I rely upon guided visualization to help people connect with their own imagery. As people close their eyes and go inside, they enter the unknown, where they receive images, sensations, and experiences. Usually, they imagine traveling to a natural setting or inside their own body. Often, instead of seeing static pictures, people experience inner landscapes that come alive and reveal meaningful clues. These clues are individualized messages that, when worked with actively, can facilitate transformation.

I usually guide people through inner landscapes by closing my eyes and entering the unknown alongside them. Rather than being specific ("See yourself at Ocean Beach in San Francisco"), I tend to offer more open-ended options ("Notice where you are. A beach? Forest?"). My intention is for people to awaken their own vision and intuition, not to follow mine. A client of seven years had me offer guided visualizations aloud because she liked my voice but almost always traveled in her own direction. Brava!

Sometimes I'm asked if, through guided visualization, people are accessing a world that exists in another dimension. There are many cultures all over the world that believe invisible spirit worlds exist. I believe energy is real and that guided visualization engages the energy body. I hold guided visualization with deep respect as a sacred experience. As such, I increase protection by creating intentional safe space before doing that work. Jyoti once told me, "If you chase the mystery, it will hide itself from you." I'm grateful for guided visualization as a healing practice. As for the rest, I'm at peace with not knowing.

Waking Up Dreams Inside

My relationship with guided visualization has grown out of personal experience. In 1994, the day after I quit law school, I opened *The Medicine Woman Inner Guidebook* by Carol Bridges and read instructions on how to meet a spiritual teacher through visualization. I had practiced traditional meditation many times before—sitting, eyes closed, focusing on my breath, and emptying my thoughts—only to feel more stuck than soothed. I needed another way in.

I memorized the book's instructions and began following them. Suddenly, the visualization came alive and I found myself entering a cobblestone cottage and sitting down on a picnic bench. I noticed a woman sitting across from me. She faded in and out like a television screen covered in a blanket of static.

Something about her felt familiar. Then I remembered. One night a couple years before, I'd dreamed I was seated on a picnic bench across from an old woman. With gray hair pulled into a tight bun, deep wrinkles, and a beaked nose, she was the most beautiful ugly woman I'd ever seen. I woke up aching to climb back into the darkness to find her. Two years later, I now found myself sitting across from the old woman in my dream. The fuzzy image smiled and said, "Congratulations, you're here. You made the right decision to leave law school. Now it's time to get to work."

So began my relationship with an invisible wise woman. It took many (many!) months of consistent practice for me to see her clearly and to decipher a connection. Her instructions were not linear, often confusing me into fits of frustration. But through her, I found my way to Oneisha Healing Tools in Half Moon Bay—a store dedicated to helping people develop consciousness—where I studied energy healing for almost five years.

The first time I met Maggi Quinlan, one of Oneisha's owners, *The Medicine Woman Inner Guidebook* lay open on her desk. With auburn wavy layered hair and blue eyes that focused into steel, Maggi questioned me about working at Oneisha. After telling her about my difficulty with meditation and my experience with the visualization, Maggi said, "That's okay. That kind of meditation doesn't always work for women because they need to be in connection. Visualization can be easier because women are drawn to being in their bodies." This offering, the first of many from Maggi, helped me identify a way of learning that my soul recognized as home.

Guided Visualization and You

Guided visualization is an essential practice I offer to help people learn how to move inward and navigate energy. Because guided visualization doesn't translate well in book form, I invite you to visit my website, *www.dancing-tree.com/book*, for downloadable audio files. I also offer individual sessions in person and via phone. If you're new to visualization, don't worry. Sometimes I feel like a curmudgeon complaining about how it took me months of sitting every day to grow my vision. Today, people don't tend to have that challenge.

Once during a women's group, a participant was having difficulty discussing spirituality because of how religion was used to hurt her as a child. As part of a guided visualization, everyone traveled through a doorway into a natural setting. Afterward, the same woman spoke up, "I got to this wooden doorway, and I couldn't open it. I kicked and screamed until I sat down in front of it and cried. Then something occurred to me. I stood up and imagined a red silk curtain. I walked right through it. I got to the other side and was at a beach, but then it was time to come back." This was her first experience of guided visualization. When she approached me afterward, I touched her arm and said, "Going from the wooden door to the red curtain? That's the shift from victimhood to empowerment. Congratulations."

Sometimes someone will tell me, "Ah, nothing happened . . ." and then share a color, sound, or image that turns out to be a *major* key to developing awareness. Learning visualization is like building a muscle; it can take time to develop. One image is a fantastic beginning and in fact, can become quite a healing gift. Through guided visualization, I've seen people cultivate intuition, clarify truths, connect with body wisdom, learn how to work with their own energy, and most of all, grow trust in themselves. Exploring inner terrain is a way to practice connecting with the unknown. The discoveries you find inside have direct and practical applications to help navigate the unknown in everyday life.

Awakening to Synchronicity

I'm thankful that when spirituality started knocking on my door as a teenager, it brought synchronicity with it. At the time, I didn't know about Carl Jung, a father of transpersonal psychology. Jung coined the word *synchronicity* and defined it as "meaningful coincidence that cannot be explained by cause and effect." All I knew was that while traveling through sacred sites in Europe with my father's community, some part of me was awakening. And the outer world seemed to illustrate these moments with a tangible punctuation mark that I couldn't ignore.

Synchronicity greeted me at our first destination in Glastonbury, England, when I connected the name Avalon on many storefront windows with the book I held in my hand. *The Mists of Avalon* by Marion Zimmer Bradley had sat untouched on my bookshelf for two years. I didn't know why I began reading it on the trip. I also didn't know Glastonbury was considered to be the nearest location of the magic island of Avalon with ancient Druidic roots. As I was catapulted into the unknown, the uncanny colliding of my inner and outer worlds propelled me to pay attention.

From there, one thing after another kept happening. The American silver dollar smacked my head on that bus ride through England. After bloodying my knee at Stonehenge, there was no scab. In the church named Briarwood, when I sobbed and prayed for my mother's eyes to heal, I felt a swirling heat encircle my own eyes. While touring yet another big church in France, I sat down in front of a statue of Mary and told her, "Look, I'm Jewish. I don't like these big cold churches. All this fuss about Jesus doesn't make sense to me. But even though religion isn't my thing and this isn't my place, I can respect you and Jesus as teachers." Suddenly, I felt a tickling sensation begin on the soft pad near my thumb and spread until my whole palm tingled. As if a switch had been turned on, my vibrating hands became a barometer throughout the rest of the trip—and in my life—for noticing when something spiritual was happening. After that, spirituality as a conversation between inner discoveries and outer realizations became a way of life.

EXERCISE: How can you begin to recognize synchronicity in your life? Contemplate events that seemed to line up and catapult you in a new direction. Look for moments when the right person called at a pivotal time, you discovered a life-changing book, or you had a chance encounter that facilitated inspiration.

Synchronicity: A Messenger of the Unknown

While I'm grateful for lightning-bolt moments of clarity, my main focus is how spirituality can be a practice for conscious daily living. And really, what does a relationship with the unknown look like within daily life, anyway? Frankly, I'm not interested in generating one-sided relationships. Are you? In the midst of all this unknowing stuff, how can we tell if Practical Spirituality actually helps?

Here, synchronicity arrives as Practical Spirituality's closest ally. As you truly begin to let go and enter into a conscious relationship with the unknown, seemingly random daily events start happening. If you can decipher how these events connect, they become a trail you can follow through the unknown. Synchronicity is a bridge, pathway, and central messenger in deep conscious relationship with the unknown. Synchronicity is Practical Spirituality's other half.

Practical Spirituality combines inner exploration with daily life awareness to expand future potential. We're going for *And* living, yes? Synchronicity can help you track progress on personal development as an outer mirror of inner life. It also offers a reality check against becoming overly focused on end results by revealing when you might be stuck. Synchronicity increases awareness by inviting you to look for meaning within daily life moments. Sometimes synchronicity can be a response to a conversation you begin with the unknown. Other times, it initiates a conversation through unexpected happenings.

The Absence of Synchronicity Can Mean You're Stuck

Yesterday, I had a conversation with "Celine." She's struggling, seeing people around her transform while she's gone through months (and months) of excruciating release work without much movement. I made the mistake of saying, "I'm so happy for them. God, they've gone through so much, they've earned this."

Then we both caught it, and Celine said, "Right. So is the take-home message that I'm doing something wrong?"

I said, "No, it's not about wrong. You're working your ass off too. But there's very little movement happening in several areas of your life. This sense of being stuck is trying to get your attention so it can teach you something. The question is, what?"

Often synchronistic events facilitate forward movement in life. The presence of synchronicity indicates flow. Celine would love to be in a relationship, but there are no prospects in sight. Her work is stagnant. Here, the absence of synchronicity reflects stagnation in Celine's life. Celine isn't wrong, but she is human. She's holding on to her hopes, dreams, and expectations about love and work with such a tight grip that there is no room for any other potential to arrive.

When you're feeling stuck and it seems like the only messages you're receiving in daily life amount to radio silence, it's time to change. Loosening your grip on hopes and expectations, which often involves grieving to let go, sends a signal to the unknown that you're open to receiving feedback. It creates room for synchronicity to communicate with you through meaningful events that can reveal all sorts of new possibilities. Here, synchronicity often begins to lead you in surprising directions where you develop trust, inner authority, or whatever healing gifts you grow (and thus earn!). If you're feeling stuck, the absence of synchronicity can communicate a lot about where shift may need to happen, both inside and out.

In addition to remaining silent, sometimes meaningful events, especially painful ones, initiate a conversation with the unknown. My friend Shira did nothing to get cancer, but she recognizes it as a call from the unknown to facilitate healing in her life. If a conscious relationship with the unknown is like a conversation rather than a lecture, communication can go both ways. As a messenger of the unknown, synchronistic events can speak volumes. It's not a matter of right or wrong. Life is change. It seems like I just gave birth to my daughter, and now in a blink of fifteen years, she's downstairs belting out a Beatles song while playing piano. And guess what she's singing at this very moment? Specifically the words, "Something in the way she moves" and "I don't know, I don't know. . . ." Is this a synchronistic wink as I sit here writing about messages in daily life? I don't know, maybe.

This raises an important question. Since it's up to each person to determine if events qualify as meaningful messages, how do we identify synchronicity? Because we are naturally attached to our view of reality, it's easy to get lost in cloudy perception. I say, if in doubt, wait. If synchronicity is trying to tell you something and you are open, it will usually keep talking. Often, I wait for three events to come together to ascribe meaning. But lightning-bolt moments can also knock my socks off. And sometimes when it seems like events are happening fast, responding quickly is important. Then following synchronicity can feel like crossing over a stream—a hop, skip, and a jump on certain stones can carry you across change to a new reality.

EXERCISE: Notice the areas in your life where you feel stuck and surrounded by unhelpful radio silence. Identify one expectation or hope surrounding this issue. Do something to begin loosening your hold—write a letter, imagine it burning, have a good cry. Then watch your daily life to see what happens.

Creating a Sacred Container

It's helpful to recognize that you're making a choice to develop a more conscious relationship with the unknown, even when you're cultivating choice within a challenging circumstance. A commitment to growing awareness is an implicit willingness to excavate beliefs, feelings, energy, and experiences from your life. If you are the first one in your family to develop awareness, part of your healing journey might include facing ancestral material. And on top of that (I know, it just keeps getting better, right?), once you do this intense work, you're most likely going to become more sensitive to others and your environment. Life will change. Remembering choice will help sustain you during painful moments when you long to hide under the covers and go back to sleep.

Just as identifying choice can support you through awakening, core personal agreements foster a sense of safety to rest into as we move forward together. Core agreements also fortify safety by creating a sacred container, an energetic cauldron to hold your process that furthers transformational healing. The time and energy you're investing to move through life differently is sacred work, at least in my book. The following agreements can potentiate your experience:

- **Be your own flavor**—making room for individual differences, including honest mistakes, will help you develop authenticity, meaning, and personal power.

- **Just keep showing up**—stay with your process one step at a time, even when it makes no sense, and eventually you'll find a soft place to land.

- **Cultivate gentle healing**—true healing takes time, so rest when you can, and if life allows, receive slowness as an opportunity to integrate learning.

- **Lean in and ask for help**—open to wise yet nonjudgmental support, including the unknown mystery itself, and realize that help may come as an invitation to change.

- **Hold your process as sacred**—allow the power of your own alchemical process to build by being particular about what you share with others.

- **Take an imaginary leap**—developing a relationship with the unknown includes inviting in play and wonder; let's get our woo-woo on together.

- **Be your own ultimate authority**—as my teacher Maggi has always said, "Feel free to leave whatever doesn't resonate on the chair when you leave the room."

Another aspect of creating a safe container involves establishing a sacred circle to hold experiential work in your designated spiritual space at home. Some basic steps for forming a sacred circle include:

1. Clearing the space energetically (burn dried herbs, use essential oil sprays, imagine a wind blowing, or more)

2. Lighting a candle (preferably a white pillar candle)

3. Invoking an invisible circle of protection by calling upon whatever is meaningful to you (the four directions, Love, the Divine Mother, Jesus, Shakti, or something else)

4. Grounding your body

After grounding, you can journal, practice guided visualization, complete exercises from this book, or do whatever you'd like. When you're finished, express gratitude and then close your sacred circle by releasing whatever you've invoked. The above steps are meant as a guide, not a mandate, so have fun and keep it simple in the beginning. Remember to put out the candle!

PRACTICE: ACTIVATING YOUR INTENTION

Go to your spiritual area and create a sacred circle using the above guidelines. After grounding, remember your intention for this book. Connect with your intention, even if this brings up fear (especially if it does!) and breathe your intention into your heart. Interact with your intention by journaling or imagining a conversation: What would you say to each other? What might your intention look like? Where might it wish to lead you? What color is it? Where does it want to live in your body? Draw your intention. Dance your intention. See yourself merging with your intention in some way. Explore. Play. Invite.

As your experience concludes, notice any sounds, colors, images, words, or textures that appeared. When you're feeling complete, express gratitude to your intention for revealing itself to you. Appreciate yourself for having the courage to show up. Close and release your circle.

A Journey in the Unknown, Together

Earth-based ways hold that when sitting in a circle, we are all aspects of each other. I've experienced many healing circles when someone had a hellish day or weekend. At some point, one of us thanks the person for all her work, acknowledging how her challenge lives in each of us and how her willingness to show up in the face of difficulty helps us all heal. We recognize that it could have just as easily been one of us facing hardship and that our time will most likely come. We also acknowledge someone who is experiencing a joyous trans-formation because, like spokes on a wheel, separation is an illusion. So thank you for how you're already showing up amidst the pain and beauty of life.

Please know that Practical Spirituality is here to be of service to you, meeting you wherever you are with love, balance, and the freedom to explore as you continue your healing journey. Along those lines, my personal intention is to be a strong, clear conduit for your learning. I'm inviting synchronicity to inform my daily life and chronicling meaningful events in real time as potential messages. We're in this together and I'm entering the unknown with you all the way.

MAPPING GUIDELINES, YOUR INTEGRATIVE QUESTIONS

- Which teachers—fear, awareness, choice, body, intuition, energy, intention, or surrender—call you the most?

- Did you create some sacred space for yourself in your home?

- Did you practice grounding?

- What are the three parts of *And* living?

- Have you experienced synchronistic events in your life? How might you welcome synchronicity into your life even more?

- Did you practice creating a sacred circle in your spiritual area?

- How can you remember your intention as you travel through this book and daily life?

3

Fear: Demons, Lizards, and Little Girls on the Threshold of Change

Fear is a powerful force that likes to come in and take over. As synchronicity would have it, fear has entered my personal life as I began to write this chapter. We just learned that in spite of our prayers and intentions, my friend Shira's cancer has reached some lymph nodes, which means further treatment. I don't know how Shira is holding this news, but my heart hurts. At the same time, another friend, Dayna Wicks, has a three-month-old daughter in the hospital in such critical condition that a heart transplant may be necessary. Yesterday, I asked my friend Maria, "Is it our stage of life or are we really in a collective shit storm of pain?" Maria responded, "We're absolutely in the shits. No doubt."

Part of me would like to pack up my family and go hide somewhere. Then I remember a lesson from Hilda Charlton, my father's spiritual teacher. She knew a family in the early 1980s who moved to an island to build a simpler, more peaceful life. Only they relocated to the Falkland Islands near Argentina just before a war broke out with Britain in 1982. The Falklands War didn't last long, but whenever I feel the urge to flee, I remember Hilda's story and what can happen when fear gets to govern decisions. Instead of staying in the present unknown, fear takes us ahead of the energy, where we usually become lost.

The same thing just happened here on the page. Instead of cultivating a pause to meet this first teacher, a fear of the pain I'm feeling for my friends moved me ahead of this book process. Perhaps I've just made a mistake in book writing. I could just hit delete, and you'd never know. But then we might miss some lessons from fear. After all, if I'm asking you to release control and consciously engage the unknown to follow energy, it's only fair that I meet you there in all levels, including how I write this book.

So as I experience my own fear-induced tantrum, as in: "Holy shit, what did I sign up for in writing this book?" I catch myself. Years of introspection have taught me that doubt screams when I'm on the threshold of change. The voice shouting at me to stop, tear up the book contract, and keep from moving farther is fear. And bingo, baby—fear is what we're here to study, yes?

EXERCISE: What's been happening in your life since you identified your intention? Notice any feelings—happy, sad, or scary. Pay attention to dreams and body sensations. Have you had any meaningful conversations or interactions regarding your intention?

PRACTICE: GROUND YOURSELF

As you welcome each of these powerful teachers into your life, remembering to ground is essential. Go to your spiritual area and use the guidelines from chapter two to create a sacred circle for yourself. Whether it's breathing into your heart, becoming a tree, or visualizing earth and star energy, cultivate a moment of conscious awareness. As you do, invite the teacher of fear to inform your intention. Begin to notice your experience of fear.

Visit *www.dancing-tree.com/book* for a free downloadable audio grounding.

What Is Fear?

Fear is an emotion based on a potentially negative reality. Fear can be a reaction to a true and immediate threat to safety. Fear can be based on a previous negative experience. Fear can also arise from a perceived threat that may not occur. Whatever the origins or truth of imminent harm, fear takes you to a future negative reality that doesn't yet exist. It's a negative reaction to the challenge of not knowing. Fear can appear as a range of adrenaline-based body sensations, including a faster heart rate, sweating, and nausea. Fear likes to come through images in the form of daydreams and nightmares. And fear *loves* to send messages through thought forms.

An extreme form of fear—the kind that traps, spins, or immobilizes you—is anxiety. Anxiety is fear of fear. The debilitating nature of anxiety requires special consideration, which I will address later. For now, just know that fear covers a range of territory.

Together, we're quickly discovering that navigating fear is very, very tricky. Fear is not your best friend or safe place, but often it pretends to be. Fear stands on the threshold of potential transformation, shouting, "Don't do it! That's a horrible idea. You're going to get hurt. Just stay here with me and you'll be okay." At first listening to fear and avoiding change seems safer, but over time, fear's overwhelming negativity makes you feel powerless. Ultimately, navigating fear means cultivating stealth so you can outmaneuver it and reclaim your power.

Many (many) spiritual beliefs and practices focus on eradicating fear. I don't believe that trying to make fear disappear by forcing it into a metaphoric closet is a good idea or, frankly, possible. I don't see fear as evil. I don't believe in removing fear to perpetuate false promises for happy outcomes. I also don't believe we can erase fear by only acknowledging love. Forcing fear into the closet may seem like we're getting rid of it, but I suspect there's some sort of secret passage that grants fear access to the basement of our lives where it runs rampant. In the process, paralyzing denial enters the room.

I propose we open the closet door and invite fear in for a clarifying conversation. Somewhere between control and surrender, we can decipher how fear may be serving us, even in misguided ways. And we may also find how fear tries to keep us safe by making us feel small. By getting to know the range of fear in our lives, we can learn how to respond rather than react unconsciously. Sometimes a response may involve tending to a fear, sometimes it may involve firmly telling fear to sit down and be quiet. Overall, fear isn't evil; fear is just scared. More important than naming every aspect of fear is learning how to work with it.

EXERCISE: How do you know when you're scared? Begin to notice how you perceive fear. Pay attention to images, body sensations, and especially thoughts.

Fear Is in the House

The last few days have been challenging. I'm walking around with a literal pain in my heart for Dayna's baby girl in intensive care. Dayna and her husband, Scott, have solid family and medical support, but they asked me to take notes at their first meeting with a heart transplant specialist.

Until Dayna called me, I had been offering constant prayers from the periphery while the most intimate family and friends held vigil. Suddenly, I was called into the center of the storm. The meeting lasted more than two hours. The kind pregnant assistant and gentle-voiced doctor compassionately walked the family through the transplant process, from describing disease symptoms and recipient selection through outlining surgery, potential complications, and post-transplant care.

I sat taking notes, breathing, and grounding deep into the earth so the waves of horrific grief would not come through me to disrupt anyone. If Dayna and Scott could listen without screaming in agony, I was determined to sit up and stay strong. In the end, I did what was asked of me, though I think the small bag of food I brought was more helpful than my note taking.

Later that evening, once the dog was fed and the kids were upstairs Facebooking, I sank onto my living room floor. Although a voice told me I didn't have any right to be so upset—this was not my life, not my child, not even my pain—I stayed with my feelings. My mouth formed a silent scream as a friend bearing witness to a living nightmare. How could this be happening? My tears flowed as a woman who recognizes unending love in another mother's eyes. How will she hold this pain? My fists pounded the floor as a human raging at the vicious reality surrounding this little girl. She's just a baby, for God's sake. I coughed and shook and sobbed as grief shredded my heart to bits. Please, please, please help them.

Afterward, I lay curled on my side for a while. Our dog, Roxie, came over and licked my face; her rough tongue felt like a kind of doctoring. I buried my head in her soft black fur. Petting Roxie helped me find balance inside. I spent the rest of the evening exhausted by sadness, recognizing my feelings didn't amount to anything but allowing them to just be.

The next morning my daughter, Kira, said, "What happened last night?"

"What do you mean?" I asked.

"You don't remember? Everyone was sleeping. It was about eleven thirty. You screamed at the top of your lungs and then Papa yelled and then Roxie barked. I had no idea what was happening."

"Wow, I vaguely remember screaming. Sorry we woke you, honey."

"Yeah, then I heard Papa going through the house with Roxie. I was awake for at least two hours after that. You scared me."

At this point my eyebrow rose to attention. Fear had entered my house in a way that didn't work for me. It was time to regroup and engage differently.

I took a breath into my heart and belly. Then I imagined myself as an old oak tree with roots planted deep in the earth and leaves kissed by the sun. I remembered my intention to explore how fear can teach people how to navigate the unknown in daily life. I also added a second intention via a message: Hey, fear, this is between you and me. Leave my family alone. Got it?

PRACTICE: YOUR INTENTION AND FEAR

Given that we have entered the unknown and fear is here, take a moment. Go to your spiritual area and use the guidelines from chapter two to create a sacred circle for yourself. Practice grounding by becoming a tree and then breathe your intention into your heart.

Through journaling, following your own imagery, or just sitting in contemplation, explore any fears surfacing in relationship with your intention. What forms have your fears taken? Notice images, body sensations, and especially thoughts. How has fear about your intention been showing up in daily life? How might fear regarding your intention relate to core fears in your life? When you feel complete, say thank you and close your circle.

Lizard Brain Fosters Fear through Resistance

I was catching up online with my favorite marketing guru, Seth Godin, when I noticed one of his blog posts about fear. Because several years ago Seth Godin had me at hello by viewing marketing as building relationship, maintaining integrity, and being remarkable, I followed the link. There I learned that his recent book, *Linchpin*, relates something he calls "the lizard brain" to fear and resistance. Because I felt synchronicity whispering (trust Seth Godin + blog post on fear + within hours of clarifying intention = potential synchronicity), I purchased his book.

Reading *Linchpin* set off a series of aha moments. In the book, Seth identifies one of the oldest parts of our brain located in the limbic system as the lizard brain—our primal side, what influences our animal-like decisions, and, it so happens, where fear lives. Seth explains how fear expresses itself as resistance through all aspects of our lives:

> The resistance is everywhere, all the time. Its goal is to make you safe, which means invisible and unchanged. Visibility is dangerous. It leads to the possibility of people laughing at you, or even death. Change is dangerous because it involves moving from the known to the unknown, and that might be dangerous.
>
> So, the resistance is wily. It works to do one of two things: get you to fit in (and become invisible) or get you to fail (which makes it unlikely that positive change will arrive, thus permitting you to stay still).
>
> [Seth Godin, *Linchpin: Are You Indispensable?* (New York: Penguin, 2010), 127.]

Seth goes on to catalog the many ways fear can express itself as resistance. In my spiritual community at the Center for Sacred Studies, we've talked about this kind of resistance for years. It's what greets people on the threshold of change and convinces them to retreat without seeking help. I can't tell you how many times I've witnessed people on the verge of stepping forward only to see them immobilized by fearful resistance. I've learned that the size and scope of this resistance reflects the potential healing people receive as they make their way through to the other side of fear. Seth agrees, "When you feel the resistance, the stall, the fear, and the pull, you know you're on to something. Whichever way the wind of resistance is coming from, that's the way to head—directly into the resistance." (Godin, 131). Identifying the nature of your resistance leads to uncovering fears. In this way, we see how fear comes through the mind.

EXERCISE: List the ways you either make yourself invisible in your life or sabotage yourself with procrastination. Take a moment to imagine life without these ways. Now list the fears that just came in, noting their form (body sensations, images, and thoughts).

Beware of Barking Dogs

Once you move through resistance and begin transforming, fear comes with you in its own way. In my world, these fears are called barking dogs. A barking-dog moment usually happens after you've moved through resistance, shown up for yourself by taking a leap in some way, and experienced something profound that most likely blows the socks off your individual electrical system. Some examples are presenting a personally meaningful idea to the public for the first time, speaking your truth to someone in your family about childhood pain, or after years of being shut down emotionally, allowing someone to hold you as you cry, shout for hours, and find new places inside.

Dogs bark as thoughts convincing you to doubt yourself and negate growth. Barking dogs can happen immediately or days to weeks after a profound experience. The thoughts begin with commenting on your process: "Wow, that was huge. I can't believe I just did that. That couldn't have happened. That was crazy. Did that just happen? Nah, I don't think that happened at all." Then over time, barking dogs get more specific: "God, I think my graph sucked. It was so unprofessional. And I was so nervous, I was incoherent." Or, "I was such a crybaby. What's the use of feeling all that? The pain won't ever end. If I go there again, it could just swallow me up." Barking-dog thoughts can be relentless.

No matter how conscious you think you are, you can't kill barking dogs. You can, however, learn to navigate them. One of my favorite sayings comes from leading spiritual author and lecturer Marianne Williamson is "Our deepest fear is not that we are inadequate. Our deepest fear is that we are powerful beyond measure." Barking dogs are a normal part of personal development. They reflect your ego complaining (loudly) as you stretch and transform. Barking dogs are just another form of fear that's trying to keep you safe by keeping you small.

So how can you navigate barking dogs? Because a barking dog is really telling you that whatever you're doing is actually working (otherwise, why would the dogs bark?), first acknowledge yourself for showing up amidst discomfort. Hey, you're practicing spirituality. Right on and good work! Barking-dog moments happen because your ego is registering a shock to your system—more like a jump start! Call in gentleness by taking time to absorb the shock. Create some space to slow down for an hour or a day or more, depending on how big a leap you've taken. Begin by focusing on one simple thing. Just breathe. Drink water. Stare at a candle flame. Pet your beloved animal. Have a cup of tea. Get a massage. Feel your body on the floor. Rest.

As dogs begin to bark, and they will, hold your focus on that one thing and just keep breathing. Don't react to the barking-dog thoughts. Just notice them. Recognize they are going to hit below the belt with some nasty stuff, and they know all your secrets. Gradually, as your ego stretches to accommodate the space you've just cleared inside yourself, the dogs will simmer down.

The next day, as the dogs approach again, maybe this time from a sneakier angle, remain vigilant. Stay close to home and cultivate quiet time—journaling, a salt-water bath, a visit with a gentle friend, or a walk in nature. Don't worry about analyzing the experience. Notice it. Over time, wisdom will emerge. So, no rush, no worries. Be firm yet gentle with yourself. Healing involves investing time, but it's time well spent.

Demons Designed to Get Your Attention

Our Western culture emphasizes a power-over relationship with the body. We vacillate between trying to control the body and denying the reality that we can't. In the process, the body becomes an object to manipulate or escape. I'm not suggesting you should or can ignore the very real pain that comes with chronic illness or a history of violation, but I do believe that shifting our relationship with the body from power-over to partnership can help facilitate healing. A conscious body fosters awareness.

A big part of my work involves helping people connect with body wisdom. Your body can become a doorway of conscious awakening to help you reinhabit yourself. This is where fear can become a great friend. In a culture that often diminishes body awareness, fear gets you to pay attention to your body through signs of discomfort. A suddenly tight belly or fast-beating heart challenges control and erases denial to awaken awareness. From there, listening to what fear has to say can become key to developing conscious relationship.

Recently, a client "Julie" came in and announced, "I need to spend this whole session on fear." This was her third meeting with me. She was seventeen weeks pregnant and had just experienced some stomach cramping and spotting. Julie was particularly upset that her practitioner had emphasized the possibility of miscarriage. Julie said, "This brought me straight into fear. My whole life, every-

one in my family goes straight into fear. I don't want to live like that."
We moved from personal processing to what I call table work, when
people lie down on a massage table, fully clothed, close their eyes,
and learn to access their own imagery and energy.

As we began guided visualization, Julie invited an image of fear
to appear. "It's a man, an old craggy man. He looks like a cartoon
character from *The Simpsons*. He's pointing to the stars and talking
about conspiracy theories."

"Does he have anything he wants to tell you directly?" I asked.

"He just said, 'You're having a miscarriage.' Hmph." Julie didn't
like hearing this.

"And look how he just got your attention by saying that, right?
This is the same guy who was just talking conspiracy theories a minute ago."

She began seeing this old man as something ancient that had
been with her for a long time. Following this imagery led Julie into
her body. "You know how some cars have those ornaments on the
hood? He sits way out in front of my heart, like a hood ornament,
leading the way. He's not bad. He's just not always right." Gradually, Julie found some healing colors that invited the grumpy man to
settle into her heart. As he did, he started changing shape, softening
into something else. We stopped there so Julie's system could settle.

EXERCISE: The next time you feel fear in your body through a sensation, follow it to the area of your body. If fear had a form, what would it
look like? If fear were a color, what would it be and where?

PRACTICE: A CONVERSATION
WITH FEAR

Find a quiet place to journal or write. Create a sacred circle based on the
guidelines in chapter two. Try grounding by breathing into your heart until
you feel peaceful inside.

Identify a fear that tends to haunt you. Open your journal and imagine you're meeting that fear for the first time. See it coming to sit across from you. What does your fear look like? Because you've never met, ask fear some questions as though you're interviewing it. Listen to what this fear has to say without believing every word. See what happens when you write a call and response, of sorts, in your journal. Perhaps fear wants to show you something. Draw it in your journal. Don't try to change fear; let it be what it is. When you've completed, thank the fear for coming. Keep writing if you want. When you're done, release your circle.

Navigating Anxiety with Energy Work

Anxiety is a severe form of fear that requires special consideration, often including therapeutic care. Because I'm not a psychotherapist or a doctor, I always proceed carefully with people, as we must be solid enough inside to open to spirituality or we risk getting lost there. If you are someone who has experienced extreme trauma or prolonged anxiety without treatment, please seek the care of a psychotherapist or psychiatrist. I do offer supplemental support to people who are currently receiving therapeutic care or who have received comprehensive care in the past. Clients with anxiety often arrive at my doorstep because they're seeking another way to work with it. Because anxiety is fear of fear, inviting it for tea and conversation can seem almost radical and perhaps terrifying. And yet, while anxiety is debilitating, I believe the amount of energy we spend trying to push it away heightens what we wish to avoid: our fear of being controlled by fear. Once it's clear that therapeutic care is taken care of responsibly, we can begin to access the energetic and spiritual dimensions of an experience.

A few years ago, I facilitated an ongoing women's group when almost everyone arrived with a previous clinical diagnosis of anxiety. At our final meeting, we discussed what we'd learned about anxiety during our two years together. The general consensus among women was how their relationship with anxiety had shifted from something bad that they needed to make go away to something undeniably challenging that they can move through. One woman said, "When my heart starts beating really fast, I go outside for a walk. I say to myself, 'This is just what's happening now. It will pass.' And eventually it does. In the meantime, I rely on my breath." Underneath the belief that it was up to these women to conquer anxiety was the judgment that they were doing something wrong. Another woman said, "Sometimes there are triggers, but sometimes anxiety just comes out of nowhere. It's not necessarily about me at all."

One woman after another compared notes about how coping mechanisms had become meaningful healing tools. Going for a run. Making jewelry. Eating nourishing food. Expressing feelings. Writing. Meditating. Remembering certain images. Playing with children. Connecting with nature. When the conversation turned to body sensations, women described physiological changes as well. A woman who used to experience anxiety as stomach cramps was now feeling tension in her heart. Another realized that chest pain had shifted to constriction in her throat. And someone else who had struggled with panic attacks for years was currently experiencing manageable heart palpitations.

As I listened to these brave, insightful women, I was reminded about what can happen when we move beyond resistance and into relationship with something, even if it's painful. In my world, sensations are just forms of energy. Out loud I said, "So what happens if we take the label off of anxiety for a minute and say you've navigated a lot of uncomfortable energy in your life?" Heads nodded silently, and I continued, "When you work with energy consciously, it can transform. Growing a relationship with this uncomfortable energy has not only taught you navigational skills, it's also shifted the energy itself." A conscious relationship with anxiety offers intense challenge and profound instruction on how to transform energy—and our lives in the process.

Lost Jewels Come through Facing Dragons

While I'm sure there are many more fears left to meet, there's a little one who has a soft place in my heart that needs acknowledging. This is not a fear that sends nasty mean thoughts into our heads or even comes as a visceral response to a potential threat. This fear does not shout. This fear has been silenced into invisibility, sent underground, and is detectable only indirectly through body sensations, nightmares, anxiety, or a lack of feeling altogether. This fear arises from trauma—some sort of physical, emotional, or sexual violation—and is usually covered in shame. Here, opening the door to imagery and energy work introduces another level of healing. Through moving slowly, survivors can meet fear within and recover parts of themselves that have been left behind.

One client several years back, "Diana," came to me with a history of clinical anxiety, bulimia, emotional abuse, and sexual violation. After many sessions, one day Diana was lying down on the table with her eyes closed, following her inner vision through a natural setting while I offered light hands-on energy work. Suddenly, she seemed to freeze and become cold to the touch. Knowing her history, I asked, "Anything in particular you want to share?"

Diana burst into tears. "I'm in front of this horrible dragon. Horrible. He's full of scales. I'm stuck in ice. I can't move."

"I'm right here. Ground. Become the tree." She liked being a tree. Slowly, we started engaging with this dragon. "Is the dragon sending you any messages?" I said.

"No, it's just standing there looking ugly." Her skin now felt warmer.

I gentled my voice. "Is there anything inside this dragon that wants to come out?"

At this point, Diana began sobbing and shaking. "Oh my God! Oh my God. He's peeling. It's a little girl! There's a girl inside the dragon!" Time stopped.

Softly, I said, "Okay, honey, let's just take this really slowly. Can you talk?" Diana nodded. I proceeded, "Where is she, this little girl?"

"She's here. We're together. But she's all curled up. She won't talk to me. She's in a little ball." Diana started crying again. I changed the music so it was soft and inviting.

I lightly held Diana's feet. "Is it okay if I say some things directly to the little girl?" Diana nodded, eyes still streaming but closed. I imagined myself as a gentle conduit of love and said, "Hey, wow, honey, thanks for joining us. We're so glad you're here. You don't have to do anything but just be here. Okay?" I paused and slowly walked around Diana, applying soft touch so she would know where I was in the room. "You know, sweetie, you just did the hardest part, you showed yourself. We're going to take this really slowly." I paused for a few minutes and then continued, "Diana? How is she?"

"She's still curled up, but I can tell she's listening." Diana was no longer crying, and her breath was now deep and even.

"Good. Diana? Send her some love, okay?" I then shifted to speak to the little one. "Hey, sweetheart, we're so glad to meet you. You're here. Take your time. We're not going anywhere. Welcome. We're just going to sit together, okay?"

It took several sessions before Diana's little girl started moving around. Often, images don't talk but show. But then the little girl told us her name. And Diana started noticing what triggers in daily life scared her little girl. Diana began integrating her little girl into everyday moments. Then little girl started offering Diana advice. Really good advice. From where I sit, Diana's reunion with her little girl marked a turning point. She began making decisions differently, including breaking up with an abusive partner. That's why whenever I encounter a fear that looks like a demon or a dragon, I don't try to kill it or make it go away. Because it could be a lost little girl who needs some love to find her way home. You just never know.

PRACTICE: MEETING FEAR

Go to your spiritual area and, using the guidelines from chapter two, create sacred space and ground yourself. Imagine walking over a threshold into a natural setting. Visit some water if you can. Find a place inside this natural setting and create another sacred circle for yourself—imagine tall redwood trees around you, draw a circle in the sand with your foot, or see a meaningful color surround you.

Next, invite a fear to come and visit. Interact with this fear, asking questions while remembering that this is your place. Notice any images, sensations, colors, sounds, or textures. When you feel ready, thank the fear for revealing itself to you. Offer it a gift and receive one in return. Release your circle and make your way back, passing the water and traveling through the threshold toward home.

Through journaling, drawing, or contemplation, review the experience. Did you recognize this fear? How does this fear arise in your daily life? Remember, just *one* image, sensation, color, or word is success. When you feel complete, close your circle and put out your candle.

Note: Do not do this exercise without support if you have a history of unprocessed trauma.

Through Fear into Awareness

Fears represent a cast of characters that range from comical, delicate, or grumpy to mean, ornery, and even malevolent. Because fear takes so many forms, it's important to proceed cautiously and strategically. Over time, as you learn how to feel your way through different fears, you'll sense the terrain that fear covers in your life. Sensing is a form of intuition.

Intuition   Resistance   Barking Dogs   Anxiety

Get to know your fears so when you're walking down a street alone at night near your home, you can decide how to respond. Recognize how fear enters your life so that when a new idea arrives and inner voices get loud, you realize you might be on to something good. Identify how *your* lizard brain expresses resistance (electronic distractions like Facebook and texting, overcommitment, or constant criticism) so you can find ways around it.

A dog barks as a thought because it's normal to react to potential change with fear. You can't kill a barking dog, but you can choose not to feed it. My father once told me, "Don't argue with fears; to do so simply makes them stronger." Trying to cage or kill fear only cements its control. In the process, you lose an opportunity to sit inside an uncomfortable unknown and discover what jewels may be hidden.

When control rules the world, fear dictates how we perceive reality. By beginning a conscious relationship with fear, you're actually freeing yourself from the hold that fear has over you. Make no mistake, you can't control fear, but you can learn to navigate fear and in the process find yourself.

While fear isn't usually your best friend, it's not your enemy either. At the end of the session with Julie, she said, "You know, I'm really glad that these stomach cramps happened. If it wasn't for that experience, I wouldn't have learned that I'm not sure this practitioner is for me. I wouldn't have met this fear and realized it's not so bad, but maybe I shouldn't always listen to it. Really, this whole thing has been a gift." In the midst of sorting through fear, Julie is learning how to cultivate awareness and make choices. She's also learning to trust—herself.

Fear covers such a broad range of emotions, and yet its most common denominator is negativity. At the same time, it seems like we aren't so good at learning through joy and bliss. Perhaps one positive result from our negative culture is that we've been wired to notice fear. From silly negative notions to terror that touches the center of our being, fear knows how to get our attention. The trick is not to be so scared of fear that we try to silence it, miss its message, or let it take control.

If you're traveling somewhere new, you might check in with fear to help you get a broader view on the landscape around you, but don't let fear be your only source of direction or you could get lost. Letting fear be the most powerful voice in navigating life narrows your conversation with the unknown.

Because fear is scary, our culture uses it as a mechanism of control by relegating it to the shadows of unconsciousness where it can run unchecked. By inviting fear out of the closet, we can shine a light of awareness and grow relationship. But here it's especially important to consider how much intimacy to cultivate. Fear tries to keep you safe by convincing you to stay small. Fear is not your safe place. Fear is more like a misguided friend who talks *way* too much, offering a steady stream of advice. It's up to you to sort through fear to find truth. In the process, you develop freedom and power.

And after you've worked through resistance and begun a conversation with fear, you enter the trickiest part of all. Because the kicker is that sometimes fear is really smart. Maggi has said "Fear isn't always your best friend, but it can be. Fear can be wisdom." Sometimes fear is spot on and becomes a key to intuition. The challenge is that because fear has cried wolf so many times, it's difficult to know when fear is not fear at all, but actually intuition.

The good news is, the more you grow relationship with the cast of characters of fear in your life, the more you'll be able to decide which fears to ignore, love, follow, or tell to sit down and stay quiet (after listening nicely a few times so they feel heard). More good news is that consciously working with your fears becomes foundational to connecting with awareness, choice, body, intuition, energy, intention, and surrender. And even better, it works both ways. As you grow closer with the other teachers in this book, they will help you navigate fear. This is especially true for intuition, the teacher in chapter seven.

Calling fear back from the past or future into the present moment in your life facilitates awakening. Listening to fear and studying where it can take you off course grows intuition. Identifying and sorting through different fears fosters clarity. From there, pieces of the puzzle of your life emerge so you can respond rather than react. A conscious relationship with fear develops awareness. And that's where we're headed next.

FEAR GUIDELINES, YOUR INTEGRATIVE QUESTIONS

- Are you practicing grounding in your daily life?

- Are you noticing synchronicity in relation to your intention?

- What ways do resistance and barking dogs try to keep you safe by keeping you small?

- How does fear tend to reveal itself to you?

- List at least three fears that regularly appear in your everyday life. Do they relate to your intention? Are your fears distinct or connected?

If no fears are arriving, especially if you have a sense of frozenness or numbness, most likely trauma is inviting you to seek professional care. Please listen.

4

Awareness: A Light Switch for Developing Consciousness

Life continues to be quite intense as I tend to my family and healing practice while writing this book. In addition to friends facing health challenges, we're also now witnessing relationships crumble. I say "we" because my husband, Alex, is here alongside me journeying through life and, thus, book writing.

Alex is exponentially more skeptical than I am. The day I first told him that I was asking synchronicity to help write this book, we were driving. In response, he rolled down the car window and said, "Hold on, honey. I'm just trying to get some air flowing in here so all the bullshit has somewhere go." We laughed hard. But then as the chapter on fear shook me up, I leaned into Alex. Right now we're witnessing how awareness can impact relationships. We're watching people who have spent decades growing children and building homes together question the very foundation of their lives. Last night, Alex said, "Their family as they know it is gone, and there's no going back. This goes straight to awareness. In one moment, their entire reality is changing." Through developing awareness, someone wakes up to a realization that has the power to change the course of a family's life. The nature of awareness shakes things up.

And in the aliveness of the writing spirit, a spontaneous moment of synchronicity just arrived: within seconds of placing that last sentence, a small earthquake shook our San Francisco house. I just checked and the US Geological Survey just reported a 3.5 quake off the San Francisco coast. I know, how crazy is that, right? My trust in synchronicity encourages me to receive this breaking news as an emphatic message regarding this teacher:

Awareness shakes things up!

Awareness has the power to change our lives on all levels. Awareness leads to questioning everything we think we know. The dictionary's listed definitions of the word *aware* include "conscious," "awake," "alert," and "watchful." Through awareness people begin investigating layers (and years) of thoughts, emotions, and experiences. Because what's hidden can feel unclear and overwhelming, developing awareness leads people into an uncomfortable unknown. The potential for change inside awareness can increase fear. If we can allow ourselves to sit in the not knowing and give ourselves permission to be with whatever arrives, learning happens. Through following awareness, trust grows in many ways.

Normally, I don't like definitive statements because I'm an *And* woman. But as a root spiritual teacher, awareness is a light switch of consciousness. It's foundational. Without awareness, people become lost in the unknown, where paralyzing denial rules and unconsciousness takes control. Sometimes, awareness can begin as a whisper. Here, awareness feels like soft air, quiet but with the ability to be everywhere, especially inside. Other times, as the recent real-life earthquake emphasizes, the force of a realization can bring you to your feet (or knock you on your ass!). This is awareness literally waking you up to a new reality or perspective.

Before we can listen to the quiet or respond to the shout, we need to enter the present moment of our lives. There, we can slow down and pay attention. In our fast-paced world, slowing down to cultivate a relationship with awareness requires effort. Like building muscle, developing awareness takes practice.

The good news is that we've already been practicing awareness together here. Learning how to notice thoughts, sounds, images, colors, and sensations engages awareness. As we travel forward, we'll step into the present moment to discuss the art of noticing. We'll explore how moving inward provides a foundation for practicing awareness and can help you develop personal tools for navigating everyday life. Finally, we'll share some stories of people utilizing these tools as a resource in daily life.

PRACTICE: GROUND YOURSELF

If you haven't already, take a moment to ground. Whether it's breathing into your heart, becoming a tree, or visualizing earth and star energy, invite the teacher of awareness to inform your intention. Begin to notice your experience of awareness.

Visit *www.dancing-tree.com/book* for a free downloadable audio grounding.

The Shift from Fear to Awareness Begins with the Permission to Not Know

There's a good reason why fear stands at the threshold of potential transformation attempting to block your way. The truth is, developing awareness involves changing. I'm not going to try to convince you that cultivating awareness is a good idea. Invite, yes, demand, no. This is your life. I trust that your psyche knows the right time for your awakening. And if not, we can usually count on an uncontrollable life challenge to arrive as an alarm clock.

Learning how to consciously hold fear helps you grow a relationship with awareness. Fear is often loud, so it's good at getting your attention. If, instead of becoming stuck in fear or control, you can learn how to see fear as a signal that something else is afoot, then fear becomes a source of awareness. Rather than yelling at the barking dog of fear to be quiet, you can thank the dog for doing its job of reminding you to stay alert for potential visitors. As opposed to being reactive, you can cultivate a sense of curiosity about what might be arriving. Then you can spend some time getting to know it and decide whether to open the door or not. In essence, the process of growing a relationship with fear is an opportunity to practice awareness.

Because fear and awareness are connected, you can also approach fear through awareness. Meaning, developing awareness will help you shift your relationship with fear and other painful feelings such as anger, grief, and shame. Awareness is the light switch of consciousness, so you can shine it anywhere to enhance learning.

Whether you're beginning with fear or awareness, giving yourself room to explore the unknown creates a vibrant foundation for learning. Rather than containing overwhelming pain or infinite beauty, what if the unknown is instead neutral? By definition, *the unknown* means "not knowing." If you can cultivate a sense of patience with not knowing, you slow yourself down. Instead of rushing ahead of something to avoid a potential discomfort, you can learn how to sit in the not knowing. You may even find a sense of peace in not knowing. It can be freeing to really not know.

Embracing not knowing creates permission to explore. To be surprised. To get creative. To find joy and magic. To face unresolved pain. This sense of permission also increases receptivity. It's not necessary to dictate a relationship to stay comfortable. Permission to explore invites a conversation that makes room for new possibilities to emerge. Letting go of the need to know makes you teachable. In the back-and-forth of true relationship, someone else leading helps you learn to follow. The permission to explore grows another level of relationship with following and navigating energy inside the unknown.

PRACTICE: BRIDGING FEAR AND THE UNKNOWN WITH AWARENESS

Bring a journal or art supplies to your spiritual area and create sacred space using the guidelines from chapter two. Write your intention in the center of a blank piece of paper and circle it. On the same page, wherever you want, write down as many fears surrounding this intention as you can. You might also draw the fear as a cartoon character, a person in your life, or just a simple color. When you're done, take a step back to look at all the different fears. Notice if any fears seem similar to each other. Then see if there is one core root fear or belief about yourself that the fears stem from. How might this core fear relate to other areas in your life?

Start a new page and, once again, write your intention in the center and circle it. Leave the space around your intention empty. Imagine that your intention is now sitting in the unknown. Notice any urges you have to fill the space. Notice any colors, words, feelings, or images that want to come in. You can write them on another piece of paper if you really need to, but allow the empty space around your intention to just be.

When you're ready, compare both pieces of paper with your circled intention, one filled with fear, the other empty. Journal or contemplate what you learned about yourself from this experience. How has noticing fear helped you cultivate awareness about your intention? How can fear surrounding your intention grow awareness in daily life? When you've completed, say thank you and release your circle.

Noticing

We are most foggy in relationship with ourselves. Just think about all the good advice you might give your friends but have difficulty accessing for yourself.

In the previous practice, you might have felt uncomfortable imagining your intention inside the unknown. Ultimately, we each need to make peace with not knowing in our own way. For me, learning how to not know is a practice of finding balance within myself. Often, recognizing that I'm off balance is what helps me remember balance. This moment of recognition is the practice of awareness I call noticing. Essentially, noticing involves paying attention to the present moment. If awareness is a light switch of consciousness, noticing helps identify some of the metaphoric rooms where we tend to hang out.

Recently, I visited with Maggi Quinlan, who advised, "Coming into relationship with ourselves means being aware of what we're feeling and thinking. Not in terms of making anything right or wrong but in terms of allowing a deeper connection both to emotions and to thoughts." Through noticing, we can explore layers of mental and emotional realms often connected to experiences that live inside us.

Because awareness takes time, it's helpful to begin with inwardly focused practices. Inward contemplation will help you begin to experience and sort through personal material. Caroline Casey, host of the *Visionary Activist Show*, says we slow down so we can speed up. Entering the present moment of a particular thought, sensation, or image grows the muscle of awareness. If you can develop awareness in the midst of internal fog, you'll be able to do it more clearly in relationship with others.

I've also noticed that many people naturally begin cultivating awareness in the context of daily life. Often it's outer circumstances that motivate a need for awareness in the first place. Because reality includes both inner experience and outer circumstances, a good recipe for awareness involves concentrated inner work as well as integrating lessons from everyday living. To help you learn, we'll explore the art of noticing in two sections: moving inward and navigating daily life.

....

EXERCISE: How do you naturally notice feelings inside yourself? What gets your attention in daily life?

....

Moving Inward

There are many ways to move inward and develop awareness, but chief among them is meditation. Honestly, meditation did not come easily for me. When I started delving into spirituality years ago, I diligently practiced emptying my mind only to discover that my

Turning Dead Ends into Doorways

inner doorway to meditation seemed to be permanently locked and sealed, in cement. Instead, when I closed my eyes and focused on my breath, experiences happened. These experiences weren't always crystal clear, but they felt alive with sensations, colors, characters, and words (instructions!) that confounded me into fits while ushering me across greater thresholds of meaning. I was too compelled to label these experiences "thinking" and push them away.

But because these experiences fell outside my understanding of what I thought meditation was supposed to be, I made myself wrong. My secret fear was that if I couldn't learn to meditate, I'd be stuck spiritually. Like Dorothy in *The Wizard of Oz* following the yellow brick road, I was afraid I might never reach home. It wasn't until I made a bent-shouldered confession of being a mediocre meditator and Maggi responded with a casual wave of her hand that I relaxed into the realization that I was already home after all, inside myself.

Today I sit across from people on healing journeys. I've been surprised at how often these people, especially women, come to me with a similar bent-shouldered confession: "I don't know what I'm doing wrong. I just can't seem to learn to meditate." I'm grateful for how guided visualization can be a gentle bridge for moving inward, especially for those challenged by traditional meditation. And I never forget that guided visualization is not the only way.

To those who believe that meditation is the only path for spiritual evolution, I say, with love, bullshit. If practicing meditation enhances awareness, wonderful. If guided visualization fosters realization, great. If yoga or mountain climbing or drawing or even picking your nose helps you move within, go for it. Ten years ago, my dear friend Sue Lockyer coined the phrase, "There's no way to do this wrong." She said this about Sacred Dance—an evening of freestyle body movement we created that still exists today—but the message applies here too. There's no wrong way to move inward. Take one step at a time, notice what's trying to get in the way of your learning (fear, judgment, shame), but don't let pain dictate the direction of your path toward wholeness.

PRACTICE: MOVING INWARD TO NOTICE

Go to your spiritual area and create sacred space using the guidelines from chapter two. If you have some instrumental music without words, put it on. After grounding, breathe into your heart and ask to awaken your observer self, the part of you who notices things. See yourself going through a doorway into a natural setting. Look around, focusing on how you perceive your surroundings. Interact with your environment as much as you wish. When you're ready, come back through the doorway. Next, draw, journal, or just contemplate the following questions:

- What did you see? How did the natural setting come alive?

- What did you sense? Did you feel an urge to explore something in particular? Did your body tingle?

- What did you hear? Did any words or sounds arrive?

- What did you feel? Did any feelings help or hinder your ability to perceive?

- What colors appeared and when?

Remember that one image, word, sensation, color, or feeling is a fantastic beginning. If any strong feeling hindered your ability to notice, draw upon the practices from the fear chapter to begin a conversation. Trust that your experience will unfold in its own right timing. When you're done, express gratitude and close your circle.

Navigating Daily Life

Some of you might roll your eyes at anything too woo-woo. A few of my clients certainly do. My intention is to find a balance between encouraging a conscious conversation with the unknown (that may involve woo-woo) and helping you integrate discoveries that empower you. To keep spirituality practical, I'm constantly investigating how practices like guided visualization cultivate tools that actually help people navigate daily life. Because many of these tools first appear as unusual images, sensations, sounds, or words, I understand the eye rolling. But to me, these experiences offer individual clues. They're messages gathered by you for you to awaken consciousness. The uniqueness of each message illustrates how we're not practicing cookie-cutter spirituality but instead are discovering authentic meaning. The following shares how some clients have turned inner work into healing tools for navigating life.

Tina

"Tina" had a clinical diagnosis of anxiety and was currently out of work on disability. She frequently experienced negative thoughts that "circled around and around," and sometimes she felt too overwhelmed to leave home. Several days ago, Tina came into our session after being immobilized for over a week. "I'm just so damn tired of being ruled by these thoughts," she said.

We brainstormed about support and then moved to the massage table for inner work. Tina took several breaths and noticed aloud, "There's this beautiful yellow light, and it's coming in through my eyes and pouring into my heart."

I said, "Okay, allow your heart to soak in what it needs." The room was quiet as I supplemented with gentle hands-on energy work.

Then Tina said, "I'm feeling pink. And all this compassion. My heart is full of compassion." Tina stayed with this for a while.

After a bit, I said, "Tina, call upon one of those thoughts that's been getting you down."

"That's easy—they come from my brain."

I placed my hand lightly on her leg for moral support. "Good. Now imagine those thoughts moving from your brain into your heart."

"They're like little black threads moving right into my heart. The colors are wrapping around the words."

"Fantastic, follow that. Allow these colors to envelop the words. Don't try to force anything. Just let the words sit inside the yellow and pink, okay?"

"Yes, and compassion is also holding the words inside my heart."

"Beautiful. Just stay with it."

Tina breathed quietly, focusing on her heart.

When it was time to end, I pulled out paper and pastels and Tina drew her experience. The colors were magnificent, and she pointed at the thin black lines, saying, "See how small those lines are? That's how small they felt inside all the color and compassion. I'm so excited, I'm shaking."

I patted her shoulder. "Shaking is energy releasing, and it's a good thing. The next time you notice mean thoughts circling round, go sit in your sacred space and look at this drawing. See if it can help you breathe the thoughts into your heart." With that, the session ended.

Yesterday, I saw Tina in a group context. Since our individual session, she'd found a new home and was deciding on paint. I remarked, "You're enjoying playing with color, eh?" She said, "Yes, color is *it*. I was in such a dark place before, but now color is coming in huge, and it's amazing. I am so much happier." While color isn't necessarily a cure-all, opening to one new thing has clearly helped Tina shift to a better place.

EXERCISE: Are you noticing any specific images, sounds, textures, or sensory experiences? How might you play with one image, color, or sound each day?

Phoebe

One day last year, "Phoebe" entered my office exclaiming, "Wait till you hear what happened!" Emanating a sense of power that had served her well during decades of corporate management, she settled into the soft armchair. "Remember how I had that big test scheduled last Friday?" I nodded. After many months of countless tests, allopathic medicine had no diagnosis for Phoebe's constant, debilitating physical pain. A holistic doctor had recommended me as energetic and spiritual support. Phoebe instinctively resonated with Practical Spirituality's no-blame approach to growing a conscious relationship with the unknown.

Phoebe detailed the preparation before the test. Fasting. Being unable to take her normal medicine to ease pain. Not sleeping all night. "This was just leading up to the procedure. I knew they were placing some kind of tube inside to monitor my stomach for twenty-four hours, but I wasn't sure what would happen." When Phoebe arrived at the hospital, she was surprised that a lab tech, not a doctor, would administer the test.

She continued, "It started with the lab tech inserting a tube through my nose, telling me to keep swallowing the tube until it was in my stomach. Staci, it was horrible. I started to gag and the tech 'assisted' by shoving the tube down my throat. I kept gagging, and the assistant was still shoving. It seemed like forever, but she got the measurements, yanked out the tube, and I thought it was over. I breathed a sigh of relief. But then she told me that now she was going to insert the real tube, the one that would stay in for twenty-four hours."

My gaze held Phoebe. "Oh my God, how horrible."

"My heart was racing. My throat tightened up. How was I going to go through this again? Then I thought about the golden gossamer wrap from our sessions. I heard your voice saying, 'You are enveloped by a golden gossamer blanket that will protect you.' Right then in the doctor's office, I told the assistant, 'Hold on. We need to do this slowly. Follow my lead.' I closed my eyes, imagined that golden glowing wrap around me, and took a deep breath. With that deep breath and the golden gossamer in mind, I started to slowly swallow, one breath at a time, bringing the tube down my throat with each breath and swallow. The tech followed my breath until the tube was in my stomach. This stuff really works."

Phoebe continued, "Oh and it didn't end there. During those twenty-four hours while the tube was in, whenever I felt nauseous or like gagging, I thought of the golden gossamer and took deep breaths, and it brought me to a place where all was well."

"Wow, Phoebe. In the midst of extreme stress, you took care of yourself. You spoke up. You accessed your intuition in so many ways. You received guidance through hearing, you saw the golden gossamer, and you relied on your breath."

Phoebe nodded. "The part about the hearing really surprised me. I always thought I was more visual, but that sentence came in loud and clear."

I said, "This is where inner work can help us navigate difficult moments. So while I'm so sorry you had this experience, you learned a lot from it."

"I'll say. And I'm going out to a fabric store to find some of that golden gossamer. I can still feel it in my hands."

"Great. And while you're searching for the golden gossamer at the fabric store, pay attention. Who knows what else may come across your path?"

EXERCISE: Have any senses arrived to help you get through challenging moments? Are they similar to senses that appear during inner work?

The *Practical* in Practical Spirituality Is You

In the midst of our busy lives, inner contemplation often takes a back seat to outward experience. But moving inward to develop awareness doesn't happen in a vacuum. It makes perfect sense for daily life circumstances to initiate the necessity of becoming more aware. You might practice visualization and then cook dinner. Or attend a yoga class after work. In this way, practicing spirituality can happen through parenting, navigating cancer, or even looking for a parking spot. The practical in Practical Spirituality comes through you.

Lightning Bolt Moments Ignite Daily Awareness

A week ago, "June" from one of my groups contacted me. We've known each other for about a year and a half. She's told me several times she was aware of a big fear she was carrying regarding health. She dropped out of college to be the primary caregiver for both her parents while they each died of cancer. Specifically, her mother died at the age of forty-five, and June is now forty-four. She has a beautiful daily life—a happy marriage, healthy kids, interesting work, nurturing friends, and solid finances—but she's been carrying the fear of cancer for twenty years. After sharing this fear with me several times, she made it clear she didn't want to do any conscious work around it, saying, "My life is good. I just don't want to go there." Following June's lead, I didn't push but just held a gentle awareness.

Of course, you can guess what happened. Sure enough, June experienced a lightning-bolt moment that unleashed fear into the center of her life. During a routine visit, June's doctor urged her, in a serious voice, to do genetic testing regarding some very life-threatening forms of cancer. Here, I don't want you to get the wrong impression. I don't believe that June did anything to invite this lightning bolt. Healing journeys occur in their own timing. Thankfully, yesterday June learned that she'd been misinformed; her genetic risk is low, so no testing is necessary.

She immediately recognized the privilege of choice about entering the unknown to develop consciousness. Instead of treating this experience as a false alarm, however, June has decided it's time to greet this fear consciously. She'll begin focused individual sessions next week.

....

EXERCISE: How might daily life present opportunities to work through old pain? What intention could help guide this process?

....

Awareness Changes Everything

Awareness changes everything. Whether inner growth or daily life circumstances issue the call for awareness, once you really wake up, life looks different. What was certain—beliefs, feelings, relationships, habits, and decisions—are now questionable. With this new perception, even the past can change shape. In this way, fear and awareness are related. Fear becomes an alarm clock for awareness to help you pay attention. Whether you hit the snooze button, react in a panic, or take a moment to wake up in a new way is your call. With fear no longer holding you back, the entrance into the unknown opens wide. The only way out is through.

Awareness also takes time to develop. As you begin to work with fear differently and accept the unknown, you create room inside. Beyond struggle, you can settle more into the unknown in order to slow down and explore. Through moving inward to notice, awareness ripens. From there, old patterns, beliefs, emotions, experiences, and whatever else needs attention rise to the surface. At first, learning to notice what's happening inside and around you may feel awkward. Remember, it takes a long time to learn how to do something well. But after a while, I hope noticing becomes a habit. And then, I really hope noticing can become your own creative practice. Through the art of awareness, you hone the ability to focus, follow, hold, and let go in your own way.

Awareness is now free to shine on all aspects of your life. Unexpected life experiences transform into awareness. And conversely, awareness transforms how you experience life. Developing awareness expands your field of perception so you can start to recognize new potential. In the present moment of expanded awareness, the possibility of choice is born.

AWARENESS GUIDELINES, YOUR INTEGRATIVE QUESTIONS

- How are you making peace with the unknown?

- What are you noticing inside yourself? In your daily life?

- What are some ways you move inward to develop awareness?

- How can you turn one image, word, color, or sensation into a tool for daily life?

- How can you move inward to explore your book intention? How is synchronicity helping you cultivate awareness via your intention?

5

Choice: Moving from Victimhood
to Empowerment

A couple days ago, I spent about two hours on the phone with Shira, my dear friend who has cancer. It was the first time we had spoken directly since before the surgery that removed her tumor and unfortunately took her rectum as well. The break in Shira's voice told me she was upset, so I silently grounded within my heart. She was at a crossroads regarding cancer treatment. Given her deep relationship with holistic healing, it's not automatic that she'll do traditional therapy. Shira was upset because she'd just received unexpected urging from an alternative practitioner to do chemotherapy and radiation. "I can handle chemo, though I'm not thrilled about it. But when I imagine my insides being fried by radiation, it feels wrong. This advice is making me question everything she's ever said. I'm really confused."

I echoed disappointment, and we discussed the practitioner. After a while, I said, "Sweetie, it's not about making specific advice, or even this practitioner, right or wrong. By gathering information from different sources, you're identifying pieces of a puzzle. But ultimately, it's up to you to bring everything together to make a decision that feels good."

And with that, Shira led me through the land of cancer, unflinchingly. She took me everywhere. From outlining statistics and the ramifications of radiation to describing holistic options and sharing dreams. My role was to ask questions and help her draw strength from past life lessons so she could explore how to hold cancer treatment. At one point, we paused as Shira expressed gratitude for the community support surrounding her. Her voice thickened into a whisper. "If there was any part of me that didn't feel worthy, it's gone. So many people have shown up to help me, there's no room for anything but love."

I drew in a deep breath and whispered back, "Oh honey, I'm so glad. And look at what healing is happening right now."

Shira breathed in deeply, and we stayed quiet for a moment. Shira said, "I don't know what I'm going to do about treatment, but I feel better." Then she shifted gears, "How's the writing going? You know, we didn't talk about fear. It's quite something." I had been observing fear and awareness during the conversation. As we spoke, an image flashed of Shira and me traveling through cancer territory in a white car. Awareness was the car itself, and while fear was with us, it wasn't sitting in the driver's seat.

I said, "I'd love to hear more. I'm just starting the chapter on choice."

Shira is a smart cookie. "Hmmm . . . choice huh? And here we are."

"Yes, my love. Here we are." While Shira hadn't made a decision about treatment, choice was on its way.

PRACTICE: GROUND YOURSELF

Take a moment to ground yourself by breathing into your heart, becoming a tree, or visualizing earth and star energy. Next connect with the teacher of choice. How can you begin to activate choice regarding your intention within and throughout daily life?

Between Fear, Awareness, and Choice

The space between fear, awareness, and choice contains potency. It's normal for fear to greet you at the threshold of change before you enter the unknown. When you can't move through fear, you sometimes retreat, become lost, or spin into a loop of anxiety. These reactions generate a sense of feeling stuck. I've received many phone calls that sound like, "No matter how hard I try, I can't seem to move forward. I don't know what to do." Life reflects stagnation pretty clearly through relationships with people, work, health, and more. Feeling immobilized can be a great indicator that it's time to let go. This sense of being stuck can be another kind of alarm clock for cultivating awareness. We seek awareness when feeling stuck becomes more uncomfortable than fearing change. Here, asking for help activates awareness and choice.

Just because you begin to develop awareness, however, doesn't mean fear disappears. Remember, fear can't be killed, and it shapeshifts as you move through resistance. What fear turns into is a whole other matter. A barking dog of fear can become a signal to check the front door of your psyche. As you investigate, fear simmers into awareness. Like Shira did, it's possible to explore and learn from a fear without letting it claim the driver's seat of your experience.

Meeting fear with awareness softens constriction. It becomes possible to notice thoughts, emotions, patterns, and experiences in a different way. Exploration grows a sense of perception. Even ordinary moments like my dog, Roxie, sleeping on her back and loudly snoring can take on new meaning. The loudness of her breath reminds me that life is precious. Her bare belly facing upward reflects trust. And her snorting helps me maintain a sense of humor! Inside the smallest detail, awareness cultivates choice. In this way, awareness and choice are essential companions. If awareness is a light switch of consciousness, choice focuses exploration in a specific direction.

Choice can indicate a sense of possibility and even abundance in the present moment. Choice represents expansiveness. Some choices are light like fairy dust while others hold the weight of the world. That's because making a choice is a demonstration of commitment. We experience choice in action. We visit with a potential new friend. We eat a turkey sandwich for lunch. We begin a different job. Choice is a practice. We hope to make wiser choices over time, but there's no guarantee. Choice is a leap of faith into the unknown. Choices can help us fly high and also crash hard. Through beauty and challenge, choice is an arrow of intention that ultimately transforms.

Choice comes with responsibility. Through Shira wrestling with treatment options we can see that conscious choice increases responsibility because it often involves stretching to hold more. The nature of stretching isn't comfortable. "Okay," I can hear you saying. "If it's so damn uncomfortable, why choose consciously?" Years ago, Maggi told me, "Life is going to present you with challenges. You can work through them consciously or unconsciously, but either way, you're making choices." Shira's conscious relationship with cancer creates more emotional, physical, spiritual, and even financial work for her. By following her process, she grows what she needs so she can choose with eyes wide open. While we all hold an intention for her complete healing, cancer doesn't get to define Shira. Instead, by choosing to grow a conscious relationship with her cancer, Shira defines herself. And therein lies a key to growing power.

As I finished writing the above, an email arrived from Shira to all of her beloveds, the first public message from her in almost a month. In it she wrote, "In making treatment decisions, I've had to really test my assumptions and resistances. I want to be open to any and all possibilities that will lead to health and ensure that cancer never grows inside my body again." Shira is leaning toward chemotherapy along with holistic care. She's also started a blog to explore "healing, wholing, holying" at *shirashaiman.wordpress.com*. Shira's embracing an *And* perspective in relationship with cancer.

Turning Dead Ends into Doorways

EXERCISE: Contemplate a moment in your life when you overcame an obstacle. Remember any fears or a sense of feeling stuck. How did you shift out of being stuck? What inner resources did you discover from this experience?

A Conscious Relationship with Conflict Generates Choice

It's one thing to learn how to choose with your eyes open wide. It's another to learn how to rest into your choices so that whether you fly or crash is beside the point. By letting go of defining yourself through an either/or reality, you develop something as precious as a great outcome: trust. Learning to trust yourself, even trust your mistakes, helps grow your power. Not power as a mechanism of control but power based on relationship.

Learning how to trust your choices depends on your relationship with relationship. You can start to assess how you're doing with relationship by looking outward. Do you have a beloved friend, spouse, sibling, coworker, or pet? Are you committed to a particular practice, cause, or way of life? Usually, we love someone or something. If not, begin a relationship with yourself.

Next, assess the quality of your relationships through examining conflict. We're starting with conflict (as opposed to peace) because we live in a conflict-oriented society. Conflict is our baseline in relationships. Here, there's a continuum of relationship that includes normal human conflict as well as unhealthy, restrictive, and violent conflict. We recognize normal: A couple argues over who does more dishes (or laundry, cooking, child care, etc.). A wife feels hurt because of her in-laws' constant criticism. Two sisters fight over who hosts Thanksgiving. A wife gets uncomfortable with her husband's drinking at her parents' house because he gets loud.

We also recognize unhealthy: A shouting husband smashes his wife across the face while their two children shrink into a corner. A woman downs her fifth shot of tequila and hurls a vicious insult at her eight-year-old son. A burly fifteen-year-old boy slams a quiet kid with glasses against a school locker, repeatedly.

Conflict in relationship doesn't have to be bad and, in fact, can fuel choice. What determines whether conflict helps or hinders choice in relationship is communication and consciousness. Frustration over division of labor in the home can lead to new insight and decisions about sharing household work. Difficult in-laws can inspire a couple to shift family visits and soften impact. Sisters can learn how to share hosting for holidays. Loud tendencies around alcohol can facilitate conversation about the meaning of quality family time. Abusive husbands, alcoholic mothers, and bullying teenagers can seek treatment and counseling to repair their relationships and their lives. When conflict meets consciousness in relationship, the potential for choice grows.

EXERCISE: Contemplate the quality of your relationships through assessing conflict in your life. What does conflict mean to you? How do you deal with conflict?

Finding Choice in the Face of Conflict Sets You Free

An obstacle to uniting conflict, consciousness, and communication is the fear of confrontation. Because most of us haven't experienced healthy conflict, we treat all friction as unhealthy, full of impending violence and unhappy endings. Confrontation may also mean accepting change. Just as we make fear wrong and push it away, we avoid conflict. Although the fear of conflict casts a domineering shadow, the decision to face the dark can set us free.

Turning Dead Ends into Doorways

For example, "Sarah's" parents consistently bemoaned their thirty-eight-year-old daughter's unmarried, childless state. Sarah wished for a family, but she also worked diligently to build a meaningful life on her own. One day Sarah met "Jack," and they fell in love. After a year, they moved in together, agreeing they were heading toward marriage and kids.

But then something changed. Increasingly, Jack cited Sarah's "negative" parents as responsible for problems in their own relationship. When Jack stopped talking about marriage, this hurt Sarah. Meanwhile, Sarah's parents expressed constant concern that Jack wasn't demonstrating real commitment. Caught in the fear that sharing negative feelings (like her parents did) would end her relationship, Sarah became unable to voice her upset to Jack. Stuck, she couldn't perceive any positive options. When Sarah's fear heightened into borderline panic attacks, she decided to seek help.

For Sarah, cultivating choice begins with developing a healthier relationship with conflict. First, she can question some of her assumptions: Why is Jack's opinion—that his and Sarah's problems are her parents' fault—automatically correct? Who made Jack the judge here? And clearly, Sarah's parents are a handful. How can Sarah develop more skillful navigation with everyone involved?

Realizing the roles that Jack, Sarah, and her parents each play transforms unhealthy conflict into a source for expansion. Conflict can then shift from something Sarah avoids into a vehicle for empowered authentic relationship with herself and Jack. From there, Sarah can reclaim her voice. Power is no longer an outside threatening force but instead becomes an inner resource to grow. Fueled from within, Sarah's relationship with power becomes rooted in trust. In moving from fear to trust, contraction to expansion, suppression to expression, the capacity for choice arrives. Sarah can then make decisions about her life through conscious relationship.

Introducing the Triangles: Your Journey from Conflict to Co-commitment

As Sarah's story shows, learning how to make conscious choices can seem like a complicated journey. Fortunately, there's a tool to help you shift your relationship with conflict and cultivate choice. At the Center for Sacred Studies we call it the Triangles.

The first triangle arises from psychologist Stephen Karpman, who in 1968 identified three roles of conflict: Victim, Persecutor, and Rescuer. Through community dialogue facilitated by teachers Jyoti and Russell Park beginning in the 1990s, four triangles emerged to help people shift from unconscious conflict to conscious relationship. Jyoti and Russell reveal these four triangles in a book coauthored with Charles and Barbara Whitfield titled *The Power of Humility: Choosing Peace Over Conflict in Relationships.* For our purpose regarding choice, we'll focus on the following two triangles:

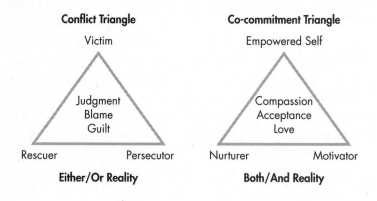

Conflict Triangle	Co-commitment Triangle
Victim	Empowered Self
Judgment Blame Guilt	Compassion Acceptance Love
Rescuer Persecutor	Nurturer Motivator
Either/Or Reality	**Both/And Reality**

These triangles represent two worlds with corresponding belief systems that impact how people relate to each other and themselves. The first triangle, the Conflict Triangle, illustrates unconscious relationships in which people compete for power to enforce one reality through the prescribed roles of Victim, Persecutor, and Rescuer. The second is the Co-commitment Triangle, which includes many realities to facilitate conscious relationship within authentic roles of Empowered Self, Motivator, and Nurturer. In the Conflict Triangle, only those in power have choice. In the Co-commitment Triangle, everyone has access to choice. As you continue on, first you'll locate yourself within the Conflict Triangle so you can find your way out. Then, through practices and examples, you'll discover how to integrate co-commitment into daily life.

EXERCISE: For easy reference, on a separate piece of paper, draw the Conflict and Co-commitment Triangles, labeling each part. You can also go to *www.dancing-tree.com/book* to download a free illustration. Post these triangles where you can see them regularly.

Conflict Triangle 101

Within the shadowy world of the Conflict Triangle, unresolved pain generates chaos through toxic relationship. It begins with a belief that resources are scarce. Two people compete to meet needs and then become locked in their own perception of reality. Because they believe there can only be one right way, people try to resolve their conflict by involving a third person, place, or thing. Survival is at stake, so lies, secrets, lack of boundaries, and a sense of *should* govern conflict.

Inside this either/or world, people relate through blame, judgment, and guilt. They take on prescribed roles where a Persecutor judges and blames to create a Victim who needs to be saved by a Rescuer fueled by guilt. Once entering Conflict terrain, people become stuck cycling through roles—a Rescuer blames a Persecutor who then becomes a Victim, while the original Victim may then turn into a Rescuer. An extreme example of cycling roles is a battering husband who victimizes his wife but when the police arrive, the wife rescues the husband from being arrested and thus persecuted by the authorities. Within groups or organizations, many Conflict Triangles can form and interact at once.

Sarah's story contains several overlapping Conflict Triangles. Early on, her parents establish a Conflict Triangle with constant pressure that Sarah's life means nothing without marriage and children. Then, Sarah's parents use guilt to pressure Sarah and Jack into marriage to save them from a grandparent-less existence. In both instances, Sarah's parents are Persecutors who turn Sarah and Jack into Victims with marriage being the Rescuer. In a different Conflict Triangle, Jack reacts to feeling pressured about marriage by blaming Sarah. He feels like a Victim but persecutes Sarah. Ultimately, judgment, blame, and guilt from every direction immobilize Sarah into victimhood.

Sound familiar? This way of Conflict, also known as codependence, runs rampant in the Western world. If you have any doubt, spend a few minutes watching any reality show on television to see how quickly you can spot the Victim, Persecutor, and Rescuer. At the same time, conflict and even codependence are a normal part of developing relationships. It's when fear and unconscious conflict take control that we end up stuck or miserable in relationships.

A Conflict in Action

As I sat writing yesterday, my twelve-year-old son, Noah, came in and sat on the couch with a bowl of cereal in hand.

I said, "Hey, babe, how are you?"

He sighed dramatically. "Hmph. Kira is a horrible person. I was just sitting next to her on the couch. She got all freaked out about her stupid camera. She even said the camera is more important than me! Well, she can just shove that—"

I turned from the computer to face him. "Now, sweetie, your sister just got that camera a couple days ago, and it really means a lot—"

"Mom, I don't care! I should be more important than some stupid camera. And now you're blaming me too! Some help you are!" Noah stomped away and slammed the door.

A few minutes later, Kira walked into the room. "What's Noah's problem today? He's such a pain."

I was once again writing and absently remarked, "I don't know honey. I thought he was fine. He liked the new summer camp."

"Well, he was eating on the couch, which he's not supposed to be doing, and I told him to be careful not to spill food on my new camera. Then he pushed the camera. I yelled at him and he was like, 'What? You love that camera more than me?' And I said, 'Yes, of course.' Then he got all dramatic and walked away."

I turned to face Kira. "Well, maybe that hurt his feelings."

Kira raised her voice. "Moooommmm, I was being sarcastic. It's not my fault if he can't take a joke. He almost ruined my new camera! You should talk to him."

Okay, I was officially paying attention. "You know, I'm finding it interesting that I'm sitting here writing about the Conflict Triangle where people get stuck in who's right or wrong, judging and blaming each other and you two are—"

"I do judge him for almost ruining my new camera because that's what he did."

"But hold on a second. Maybe you both have a point. You were protective about your new camera and maybe you hurt your brother's feelings. There's room for more than one view of reality, Kira."

"Oh no, no, no. There's only one reality here, Mom. He shouldn't have been anywhere near my camera. You should go tell him to be more careful."

Clearly, my kids wanted me to referee. But since they're usually close (and I have a relationship with the Co-commitment Triangle!), I ignored the temptation to intervene and said, "Honey, I trust that if you go talk with him, you two can work this out together."

"He's the one who overreacted, not me. I'm not going to say one word until he apologizes even if we don't talk all night long! Thanks for all your help, Mom!" With that, she stomped away.

I wish I could write that my children ended their conflict through a peaceful, validating discussion. Instead, Kira offered Noah juice at dinner, and Noah reciprocated with a compliment about the fish she cooked. Then they joined forces to bargain for leftover chocolate cake. No groundbreaking heartfelt moments, but chocolate is always a good beginning.

EXERCISE: Contemplate a recent disagreement you've had with someone in your life. Were you arguing about competing realities? Did you feel judged and blamed? Or did you do the blaming? Where was guilt in this dynamic? Did you try to fix the situation by taking on too much?

Spotting Conflict Triangles in Your Relationships with Others

Discovering that the Conflict Triangle lives in your relationships means that you're human, not evil. Just as meeting fear is helpful, noticing your inner Victim, Persecutor, or Rescuer increases awareness and activates choice. Let's pretend you're a detective examining relationships in your life. There are a host of clues that help you recognize a Conflict Triangle. Please remember we're creating healing tools not a whip for beating yourself, okay? Here are the clues:

1. **The Conflict Triangle needs a good Victim.** A big difference between a Victim and someone who has been hurt is not the absence of pain but how the pain is held. In the Conflict

Turning Dead Ends into Doorways

Triangle, Victims feel powerless against the people, feelings, and circumstances surrounding them. They feel they have no freedom or choice. Victims often feel stuck. What distinguishes a Victim from a survivor is the perception that there is no way out. A Victim has somehow signed on to an either/or perception of reality.

In the above example, both my children fought over the role of Victim. My daughter perceived that her new camera might be a Victim of my son's food spillage, and my son felt like the Victim of his sister's cruelty. Clearly, my kids are expressing normal sibling conflict. But that's the point. Within the continuum of healthy to unhealthy conflict, we can all relate to victimhood.

2. **Only one reality stands inside Conflict.** Conflict can become unhealthy when people believe there's not enough nurturing for everyone. With so little room, individuals invest in their view to survive. Reality becomes distorted. Russell Park illustrates this distortion in his story about six blind East Indians describing an elephant:

"The one in the front [of the elephant] says, 'Well, the elephant is like a fire hose,' and the one in the back says, 'No, it's like a long rope with a tassel at the end,' and the one at the leg says, 'No an elephant is like a tree stump.' And they're all absolutely right with the piece of the elephant they've got. But of course, none of them sees the whole elephant. That's the same way reality is. None of us can see the whole thing, but what happens is we believe that ours is the correct reality and we start arguing and competing for it" (Russell Park, interview by Staci Boden for master's thesis, *Dancing with the Shadow: Transformational Pregnancy as Practice for Living Daily*, November 17, 1997).

Insisting on one right way makes everything else wrong. Reality splits into an either/or dualistic perspective. Whatever isn't black and "good" is white and "bad." With no room for shades of gray, secrets and lies persist. Survival dictates pushing the bad away, onto someone or something else. From there, judgment is born.

3. **Judgment and blame run wild in the Conflict Triangle.** Moral questions aside, there's a difference between discerning what feels right for ourselves and imposing that view onto another person. Making someone else wrong transforms discernment into judgment. Judging others further cements an either/or reality to intensify conflict. In Sarah's family, the judgment that marriage is the only way to demonstrate commitment threatens her relationship with Jack. My children threw daggers of judgment and blame to establish a claim over one reality. When judgment or blame is in the air, most likely a Conflict Triangle is in the house.

EXERCISE: After identifying one relationship or situation where you feel stuck in the Conflict Triangle, take a broader view of your life. In contemplating many relationships, what role of Victim, Persecutor, or Rescuer do you most often repeat? Look to your childhood for patterns and notice birth order, gender issues, family dynamics, and life experiences. Don't judge, just notice.

---

4. **Guilt and *should* fuel Conflict Triangles.** In a singular reality, whoever maintains the monopoly of power establishes "right" and "wrong," "good" or "bad." Many of us with a Jewish or Catholic background are genetically wired to recognize guilt: a twisting sensation that rises from the pit of our stomach demanding we do something good or berating us for being bad. In a Conflict Triangle, guilt becomes the currency that manipulates people into roles and action based on *shoulds*.

For example, Sarah's role as Victim is solidified through guilt and *shoulds*: Sarah should be married with children; she should not be like her negative parents; she should leave Jack (or get him to marry her) so her parents don't have to die grandchildren-less. Additionally, Conflict Triangles form when two people caught in a painful dynamic reach out to a third party with a *should* attempting to create a Rescuer. Both my children used guilt and *should*s to draw me in (welcome to the pitfalls of motherhood!). Guilt bites hard.

5. **Ring around the Rosie, Conflict Triangle style.** In an atmosphere where only one reality rules, people suppress feelings, thoughts, and actions to survive. With no room for authentic expression, the only movement comes from circling through conflict roles. As people spin through one lose-lose dynamic after another, they turn other relationships into Conflict Triangles in an effort to somehow break free. In fact, they often reenact one specific role across many situations. Once we're stuck in a Conflict Triangle, ashes to ashes, we all fall down.

   Both my children saw themselves as Victims, but in blaming each other, they became Persecutors. I could've intervened as a Rescuer to one child (Noah's wrong for eating on the couch, or Kira's wrong to care more about a camera than kindness) only to be a Persecutor of the other child. If I had entered as a Rescuer, I could've become a Victim myself, feeling judged and blamed by both of my kids (which they tried to do anyway).

EXERCISE: Do you have a loud inner bully? Or often feel paralyzed by life's circumstances? Do you take on too much to maintain the status quo? Which conflict role do you lean toward?

Acknowledging the Conflict Triangle Within

While triangles take residence in our relationships, these conflicts live inside us as well. We internally cycle through roles within the

Conflict Triangle, judging our own thoughts and life choices, large and small.

For example, I'm contemplating eating a tantalizing piece of chocolate cake:

A mean thought snarls, "What are you, stupid? Don't do it. You're already five pounds up. And by the way, if you think that sitting around on your ass all day writing is going to help matters, get real."

Another thought chimes in, "Hey, don't talk to her like that! She's working hard, and she needs to let off steam. One piece of cake isn't the end of the world. Besides, it's Friday."

The first voice argues, "What do you mean. 'It's Friday'? That's an idiotic excuse. Don't you know that chocolate cake is just the beginning?"

The second voice raises, "Don't talk to me that way! And stop trying to scare her. One piece of cake is not the end of the world. She exercises five days a week."

I chime in, "Hey, actually, I really don't want the cake. Sugar makes me cranky. Stop trying to get me to eat crappy food."

The second voice sniffs. "Fine, don't have it. Even though your great-grandmother would say it's bad luck not to eat your son's birthday cake. And Happy Friday to you, too."

Sound familiar? Begin noticing how many times a day you spin through Persecutor to Victim to Rescuer. Most of us are experts at relentlessly beating ourselves down with judgment and blame. Like fear, the Persecutor tries to keep us safe by keeping us small. Also notice how the Rescuer sabotages potential empowerment.

Spotting conflict roles in relationships with others can be a starting point, but remember that these outer dynamics mirror an inner relationship. Our core relationship with ourselves—whether our role is Victim, Persecutor, or Rescuer—is often what we project outward onto others. Jyoti reminds us, inside, outside, same side. And while we may lean toward one variation, remember the Conflict Triangle will spin you through all three roles in a lose-lose dynamic.

EXERCISE: Pay attention to your inner voices for a day. What role do you most often take in relationship with yourself? How do your outer relationships reflect this dynamic?

From Conflict to Co-commitment, Choice in the Heart

After learning about the treacherous terrain inside a Conflict Triangle, wouldn't you like to live somewhere else? In *The Power of Humility*, authors Charles Whitfield, Barbara Whitfield, Russell Park, and Jeneane Prevatt envision a new paradigm of co-commitment "based on cooperation, positive thoughts and relationship patterns of support, respect and responsibility for one's choices." Teachers at the Center for Sacred Studies locate the Triangles in different parts of the body. The Conflict Triangle sits in the lower areas of the body governing survival, passion, and mind/ego, while the Co-commitment Triangle lives in the heart. When we shift our center of gravity from conflict to co-commitment, we travel from a constricted state of victimhood to a heart-centered, empowered way of life.

In the nourishing world of co-commitment, confined roles transform into pathways for self-realization. The Persecutor becomes a Motivator, someone who observes without judgment and blame. The Rescuer shifts from fixing through control to being a Nurturer who helps the Victim identify needs and discover choice. Through this process, a Victim finds a voice to grow inner authority and become an Empowered Self. Choice thrives alongside empowerment.

Ultimately, while awareness can help locate what triangle you're inhabiting, moving out of conflict and into co-commitment requires constant choice. Through practicing what you most need to learn—making a choice—you develop the ability to sustain a co-commitment way of life. You can make a choice to remain authentic and empowered every day. The following provides helpful clues and practical insight for embodying co-commitment within and throughout daily life.

1. **Don't be trapped by a narrow perception of reality.** Instead of being like the six blind East Indians using a narrow view to describe an elephant, recognize that reality comes in many shapes. Making room for more than one reality releases the trap of an either/or view and introduces awareness of choice.

   Here, it's important to acknowledge that for people living with challenges like chronic illness, disease, or financial stress, reality may have undeniable limitations. The journey becomes how to find choice inside a challenge. A major clue begins with shifting from being a potential Victim who feels powerless to an Empowered Self who identifies feelings and needs. When Sarah noticed her fear intensifying into panic attacks, she realized it was time to seek help from a nonjudgmental source. Shira's honest distress about radiation motivated her to integrate allopathic and holistic treatments, redefining healing for herself.

2. **Release judgment, blame, and guilt and kiss *should* goodbye.** The antidote to a *should* existence begins with letting go of other people's perceptions of reality and releasing the negative habits of judgment, blame, and guilt. Shifting these patterns takes practice. Recently, Jill Pettegrew, who co-facilitates Sacred Dance with me, suggested a Buddhist practice of invoking compassion, acceptance, and love in place of the more familiar negative patterns in life. As a beginning place, choose a specific judgment and see what happens when you invite compassion, acceptance, and love.

EXERCISE: Contemplate a challenging relationship. What does your heart need? Notice what comes without taking action.

Turning Dead Ends into Doorways

3. **Invoke co-commitment through a loving *I*.** How does conscious communication work in the Co-commitment Triangle? A key to speaking from the heart begins with *I* statements. Rescuers make no presumptions and learn to be Nurturers by asking the Victim, "How can I support you?" Victims become Empowered Selves by identifying their needs. Persecutors transform from a pointed finger into Motivators by noticing: "Wow, I'm feeling frustrated. What's happening with you?" Motivators also cheerlead creative potential: "So you're telling me you're angry, and I'm frustrated. I bet we could come up with another way to do this. How about . . ." By the way, "I feel that you're being a jerk" is not an *I* statement; it's a *you* statement of judgment.

In the Co-commitment Triangle, people speak their truth from where they sit, and all perspectives are welcome. As you begin to peel away *shoulds* and access feelings, your authentic self will emerge. Please remember to cultivate a safe place in sharing these new parts of yourself with others.

PRACTICE: YOUR INNER CONFLICT AND CO-COMMITMENT TRIANGLES

Go to your spiritual area with a copy of the Conflict and Co-commitment Triangles and create a sacred circle. Imagine you are traveling inside your body to visit your inner Conflict Triangle. Interact with whatever role of Victim, Persecutor, or Rescuer comes forward. How has this role gotten in your way? How has it protected you? What does it need to heal? Do this with all three Conflict roles.

Next, find your inner Co-commitment Triangle. Invite your Empowered Self to step forward and connect. Ask your Empowered Self to give you a tour of your inner Co-commitment Triangle. It's okay if it isn't a utopia. What needs to happen so you can fully inhabit this place? Offer a gift to your Empowered Self. You can meet your inner Motivator and Nurturer as well.

When you're ready, see if anything wishes to come back into daily life with you. Journal, contemplate, draw, dance, sing, or do whatever is meaningful to remember this experience, noticing any particular images, sounds, words, colors, or textures regarding your Empowered Self, Nurturer, or Motivator. Close your circle when you feel complete.

Navigating Conflict Relationships from a Co-commitment Perspective

As you notice Conflict Triangle relationships and grow authenticity, unconsciousness inevitably becomes more painful. Judgment and blame may start to feel toxic—your body might even have a physical response. You'll naturally begin to sort through your relationships and sift according to levels of toxicity that you can handle. Conscious choice is becoming more active in your life. Some people may fall way. Other people may be stuck in conflict but remain part of your life. Does this mean that when you're together you're going to be dragged back into the Conflict Triangle? Dragged maybe, tested definitely. So how do you stand your ground inside co-commitment?

1. **Stay true to your *I*.** You can carry *I* statements into any situation, including Conflict Triangles. If someone is blaming, say how you feel. Make an observation without judgment, as in "I'm noticing some anger here." When faced with a Victim, a Nurturer can say, "I'm really sorry for your pain. This seems like a challenging situation. How can I support you?" If well-meaning people are trying to turn you into a Victim by throwing a pity party, you can stay empowered with, "Yes, I'm sad about what's happening. My heart hurts. I'd really like a hug." Staying with *I* statements helps you avoid the pitfalls of judgment, blame, and guilt. They help you maintain your authenticity in the face of either/or and *should* perspectives. Notice how dynamics change when you approach a conflict moment with co-commitment skills. Shift happens, baby!

2. **Embrace boundaries and the right to be wrong.** Most groups, families, and work environments thrive on Conflict Triangles. The basis of triangulating to third parties in reaction to unconscious pain (usually from childhood) comes from unhealthy boundaries. Everybody is up in everyone else's business, judging, blaming, and speaking for each other. In an atmosphere where realities coexist, authenticity emerges as personal truth. Individuality is not a threat to the survival of a group but is instead an avenue for expansion. Difference becomes a valuable resource to recognize, cultivate, and celebrate. Through group support, individuals identify needs and discover their own sense of balance. Healthier boundaries are born.

This is where navigation gets a bit tricky. A Conflict Triangle experiences healthy boundaries as a threat. A Rescuer must sacrifice individual truth to maintain the status quo. If a Victim learns how to identify needs, there's no one to persecute or rescue. People within the Conflict Triangle may test you by trying to tear your healthy boundaries down. You will be made wrong. This is where it's important to speak your truth. It's not about you determining what's right for everyone, just what feels right for you in any given moment. Resist the temptation to defend yourself or make the Conflict Triangle wrong (because if you do, gotcha, you're back in conflict). Remember, you catch more flies with honey. So hold your boundaries firmly, but also remember love, acceptance, and compassion. You'll have many opportunities to practice maintaining boundaries in a way that works for you.

Intimate Individuating: Death Becomes Rebirth

For the most part, as you develop consciousness, you will be able to navigate unconscious dynamics more successfully with most people in your life. After all, it's not on you to cure the world of conflict. The intention is for you to cultivate choice. This may not be so easy with your most intimate beloveds such as a partner, parent, sibling, or best friend. Once the veil of conflict begins to lift, the cost of tolerating toxicity to maintain an unhealthy status quo may be too high to bear. At this point, challenges can appear with people who are content to live inside the Conflict Triangle. These beloveds are in a different place in their process. Most likely, they are standing at the threshold of change, stuck between denial and fear.

If you decide to speak up, your voice will make waves. In larger family dynamics, multiple levels of Conflict Triangles may be in play. You may face a sea of judgment, blame, and guilt. You could be told to shut up, to stop destroying your family. People may call you a crazy troublemaker, and they may enlist others to talk some sense into you. You may be ostracized. Emergencies may suddenly happen that only you can fix.

Please know that I'm with you at this painful time. As a person who's initiated change and been initiated by change in relationship, I've been on all sides of this experience. I've mentioned that Alex and I are witnessing relationships negotiating this territory. Children are involved, and the stakes are high. Something is in the process of dying. You may find yourself grieving over the potential loss of a relationship, the painful reality you tolerated for so long, and also the dream you hoped to manifest that never arrived. You've reached a choice point in relationship, and the only way out is through. Here, remember that death does not have to be a final ending but can be a portal for rebirth. In other words, just because a form of relationship needs to die, it doesn't mean the relationship is over.

This is a moment when you need to call upon all your courage to stay with your process. To trust what's unfolding even though it may be leading you places you never imagined or wanted to go. Ground, breathe, and take one step at a time, resting when you can. Call upon compassion and resist the impulse to make your beloved wrong. If you're the person initiating change, remember that being able to pause for an in-breath at the threshold of consciousness makes you privileged. If you're feeling shocked (or betrayed) by unfolding events, I encourage you to open to the healing potential at hand.

In most situations, we all have a mistake to claim and a lesson to learn. Everyone involved is most likely expressing some form of an unconscious wound. *Unconscious* just means "unknowing"; you can't be aware of what you haven't learned. It's normal to need help during this time, so make sure to seek conscious support. May you find the strength to recognize that through this death process, you have the capacity to rebirth yourself. Just keep showing up.

To rebirth your relationship, there are many points of navigation:

- Receiving each other's truth as an invitation to change and answering it with every fiber of your being

- Sitting in the unknown and holding fear while letting the form of your relationship really die

- Allowing yourself to fully grieve the death of your current relationship, including any hopes or expectations it carried

- Traveling inside your experience to excavate root wounds so they become compost for conscious change

- Staying in the unknown, without any expectation about what this relationship may or may not look like in the future

From here your relationship might rise like a phoenix from the ashes in a whole new way.

There are other avenues that point toward a more definitive ending:

- Being unwilling to change

- Feeling done with each other

- Damaging toxicity that severs connection beyond repair

- Lacking the emotional capacity to show up and do the work

- Being unable to tolerate the level of the unknown everyone needs to hold

It may help to remember that this outer experience is mirroring an inner process. Or that regardless of what happens with this specific relationship, moments of individuation hold the possibility of birthing another level of development. Please know that my heart is with you at this time. Rest when you can and call in gentleness, okay?

Everyday Choice Nurtures Meaning

The day I began writing about the Triangles, I received a letter from a family member who's never sent me anything directly before. It was a brief article in *Ode Magazine* by Paulo Coelho, a powerful author of many profound books including *The Alchemist*. The article is titled "How I Write: Why Writing a Book Is One of the Loneliest Activities in the World." In it, Coelho describes his writing process as starting each morning with fear, procrastination, a sense of *should* and lasting until "this feeling of guilt" propels writing around dinnertime. Of course, that's when he merges with a writing force that carries him deep into the night as he explores "the unknown sea" of his soul. The next day, the pattern is exactly the same. He states, "But that's the way it works. There is no other way."

Reading Coelho's truth about his relationship with writing helped me shift mine. The level of energy required to write a book is no joke. The chapters on fear and awareness threw me off balance, asking me to hold holy-shit moments as I met new levels of vulnerability inside the unknown. When I was honest about how raw I felt, a couple of people in my life pushed, "But aren't you enjoying this book-writing process?" I began to hold this question.

Receiving Coelho's article made me realize that my holy-shit moments were not only shouts at the threshold of transformation but also a Victim's cry. Here, the question of whether I'm enjoying writing this book can taunt me into an expectation that I should. That somehow writing this book needs to look a certain way.

Instead of caging my experience inside a particular definition of *enjoy*, I'm trusting authenticity. My friends aren't wrong for asking the question. I can reflect on a full range of emotions in response. I then free myself to sit in the intensity of my body throbbing with an ecstatic pain as these words pour from my heart onto this page. I take a deep breath into the present moment and feel how much I love intensity. It isn't a first-blush, la-la land, euphoric kind of intense. It's a squishy, heartbreaking, open, raw, surprisingly wild, faith-growing, lightning-bolt-of-awakening kind of intense. My perspective broadens into gratitude for the privilege of sitting here writing a book that was planted inside long ago. As I give birth to words, I grow myself. From here, the many ways I can enjoy writing this book becomes full of possibility to learn.

PRACTICE: EXPLORING INTENTION IN LIGHT OF CONFLICT AND CO-COMMITMENT

Go to your spiritual area with a journal or drawing materials, and create sacred space. Consider your book intention as a relationship. What conflicts are you having with your intention? What either/or beliefs might be getting in your way? What conflict role are you in relationship with your intention (Victim, Persecutor, Rescuer)? For help, look at the earlier practice when you drew fears around your intention; also examine judgment, blame, and guilt. What do you need to shift your relationship with your intention?

Imagine your Empowered Self and your intention meeting within your heart. See them taking a walk in a natural setting or meeting for tea and conversation. What gifts can they exchange? Next, invite your inner Nurturer and Motivator to join you. How can they support your intention to enter your daily life? Ask to be shown and then notice any images, words, colors, senses, urges, or feelings that arrive. Spend a few minutes drawing or journaling one thing you perceive. When you're done, express gratitude and close your circle. As you move through daily life, begin activating an empowered relationship with your intention.

Holding Choice as a Healing Path

Last night during a group, someone shared a story. "As I was driving over, I was thinking about life. About how so-and-so's done me wrong. And in the past, I would've gone there. Hell, I would've gone there and I would have fed it, making it bigger and larger until it became this huge story that consumed me. But this time I caught myself. 'Ha, Victim.' And then I said to myself. 'Nope. I'm not going to be a Victim in my life. No.' Then I just let the story go."

As I listened, chills went up my spine and my intuition shouted, "Yes!"

The heart of shifting from conflict to co-commitment happens through practicing choice. Realizing we hold the key to our own empowerment can change everything. Does moving from Victim to Empowered Self automatically transform reality? Not necessarily. But the ability to invite choice by asking, "What do I need?" and "How can I support you?" in any circumstance opens the door to a friendlier unknown. Jill Pettegrew recently said, "Sometimes miracles show up as a shift from inside." Learning how to shift involves a conscious choice.

Jyoti teaches that when faced with seemingly distinct parts of our lives—health issues, a great job, financial challenges, or a heart's desire—we must hold each of them. She sits with her hands in front of her heart, holding her palms upright until they face each other a few inches apart, like an open prayer. "As you keep holding," Jyoti says, "these parts will start to move." Then she begins to rotate her hands forward, wrists arching down, palm still facing palm. "As they move, these parts of your life will rearrange themselves and come together as a new form." Her fingertips touch so that her hands look like an arrow. "And then, the energy generated from holding these points carries this new form into the future." With that, her arrow hands move from her heart and fly into the air, touching each person in the room.

It's one thing to sit in an unknown and hold parts that are full of beautiful potential. It's quite another when the unknown contains a threat of loss. An intention to heal might mean holding cancer, allopathic medicine, and holistic modalities together. Embodying authenticity might involve learning how to face fears and speak our truth about intimate relationship even if it means disappointing people we love. Sometimes the choice not to collapse into numbing denial, the choice to remain awake as all the distinct parts of our lives transform, hurts like hell. But as a practical woman, I'd still rather sit in the present moment with a painful unknown and cultivate possibility than avoid pain by rushing toward a certain death.

A conscious relationship with choice teaches us how to hold the pain and the beauty of life alongside each other. Sometimes life needs us to choose quickly. Other times, the choice to consciously hold conflict inside the unknown without doing anything potentiates another level of transformation. It's through holding this way that we can learn how to stay behind the power of whatever is transforming so that when the seemingly discordant points meet, as Jyoti describes, nothing blocks new form from taking flight.

In choosing to work with an intention in this book, you're consciously holding parts of your life so they can interact. The new form that emerges may or may not be a tangible outcome, but most likely it will mirror something you need to learn—patience, wisdom, inner authority, receptivity, creativity, and so on. In this way, you're growing a new level of trust inside so you can become responsible through your own awakening. There is no greater awakener than the body. With the power to initiate life and death, body is the ultimate source of transformation.

CHOICE GUIDELINES, YOUR INTEGRATIVE QUESTIONS

- What helps or hinders your ability to make choices in your life?

- What's your relationship like with conflict?

- Do you have the two Triangles posted somewhere you can see them daily?

- How do you recognize a Conflict Triangle in action?

- Do you tend toward Victim, Persecutor, or Rescuer in relationship with others? What about within yourself?

- How do you recognize a Co-commitment Triangle?

- How can you become an Empowered Self, Motivator, and Nurturer? Here, remember to ask: What do I need? How can I support you?

- How can a conscious relationship with choice help you activate and follow your intention?

6

Body: The Ultimate Doorway for Awakening Consciousness

About two weeks ago, I sat with my teenage daughter in an alternative doctor's office discussing her test results. For years, Kira has had strange reactions to food and substances that allopathic medicine can't explain. She can't seem to eat a simple meal or brush her teeth without several minutes of sneezing afterward. Lately, an irritated stomach interferes with breakfast. While the kind and intelligent doctor talked to Kira, I remembered my father sitting next to me in a similar office as I discovered a gluten/wheat allergy on the cusp of fifteen. At that time, there were few alternatives to wheat, so I carried cardboard-like, crumbling rice cakes throughout high school and college. As Kira took in the news that she was allergic to cow's milk, I marveled at the body as teacher. Staying off gluten during such formative years facilitated awareness. Was my daughter on the threshold of body as a doorway for awakening consciousness?

Then the doctor addressed me, "As sensitive as your daughter is, you're infinitely more allergic to cow's milk."

I sputtered, "Me? What? But I don't have any reaction to—"

"A milk allergy is different than an intolerance and might not produce symptoms. You won't know until you eliminate milk from your diet completely."

"What?! Now, hold on. I just got tested to be supportive. There's no way in hell I'm giving up milk in my coffee."

Kira nudged my arm. "Aw, come on, Mom. It won't be that bad."

I breathed in and reminded myself I was supposed to be the parent. "I'm just having a moment. Kira, why don't you go get that snack while I get these results, okay, honey?"

About halfway through my meeting, the doctor put down his pencil, stared pointedly at my arms clenched tight across my chest, and said, "You know, what you do with this information is your choice. This is your body."

Fear, awareness, choice, body. Bingo. The big energy of body had arrived. Who might be on the threshold of a conscious awakening? I uncrossed my arms and replied, "I hear you. Let's continue."

PRACTICE: GROUND YOURSELF

Imagine an invisible circle of support, ground yourself, and recognize body as a teacher in your life. Remember your intention and notice if it relates to your body awakening consciousness in some way. How might your body already be informing your intention?

Body as the Ultimate Doorway of Transformation

Two weeks after meeting with the doctor, my daughter and I are off cow's milk while my son and husband are wheat/gluten-free. Rather than eating sugar, our kids find joy as Alex turns mixing sixteen ounces of nutritious green plant goo with fish oil into a comedy, which usually ends tragically as he quotes an ironic truth: what doesn't kill you makes you stronger.

The first week off dairy, I might've traded my husband for a slice of cheddar cheese. By the second week, feverish sampling of soy, coconut, and almond milk faded into sad longing as I sipped my fake cream–filled coffee. At the same time, while I moaned a bit, I didn't get stuck in a Victim's cry. When a friend remarked, "So you invited in body as a teacher, and now your whole family is in detox?" I raised a glass of water in salute and answered, "Oops." The truth is, I'm not sure if what's happening is synchronicity regarding the book or just the prevalence of body in daily life. And it doesn't matter. As I've researched dairy- and gluten-free dinners while watching my teenage children choose diligence over deprivation, I'm already grateful.

Around me are people who don't have the luxury of merely giving up milk to fine-tune their quality of life. At this very moment, my friend Dayna sits in the hospital beside her baby daughter Dyllan, now seven months old. Yesterday, Dyllan had her second operation in the past week to receive a mechanical heart to keep her alive until a real heart becomes available for transplant. Dayna and Scott are not only witnessing their baby's life hanging in the balance while coordinating round-the-clock hospital volunteers to support Dyllan, but they also juggle care for their four-year-old daughter at home. While I don't presume to know for sure, it's pretty clear that Dyllan facing a heart transplant is not a gentle initiation of body as teacher.

Elsewhere, as I support clients in my practice, I'm witnessing how the trauma of buried sexual abuse can haunt people. I'm noticing how trauma damages trust and severs adolescents from developing power. Decisions become reactive, often reinforcing people's denial to cope with life. Left untended, trauma recycles into anxiety, addiction, insomnia, nightmares, eating disorders, abusive relationships, and more. Here, healing often involves meeting the original trauma at its source—through the body—to reclaim oneself.

I also seem to be surrounded by the fruitful bellies of pregnant women, a few who are close friends and family. I'll even be dusting off my former professional doula skills to attend a birth later on during this book journey. Whether a woman ends up birthing a baby or not, engaging fertility invites another level of relationship with the body. Fertility leads people into the heart of desire and the center of the unknown because, with all its machinations, technology cannot guarantee life. There's no way around the truth that body creates life.

What personally sustains me through the current waves of intensity, besides my beloveds and a cup of coffee, is body movement. As a chunky teenager, dance taught me to nourish health and embody pleasure. Today, dance is my primary spiritual practice, showing me how to receive, express, and follow daily unknowns through creative play.

Food challenges, sick babies, sexual abuse, and abundant fertility remind me about the body's capacity for awakening consciousness. Discovering fear, navigating health, identifying inner tools, and cultivating choice all involve a relationship with body in some way. My mentor Jennifer Sugarwoman has stated, "Body isn't just a doorway, it's *the* doorway." Another teacher, Maggi, explained, "I always come back to the body because it is the vehicle that will take us there. Whether it takes us through deliberate inward turning, breathwork, dancing, food, accidents, illnesses, pregnancy, or even death . . . it doesn't matter. Everything we do is an opportunity to go deeper into ourselves and eventually peel back enough layers so we can connect with spirit and access healing."

As the gatekeeper of life and death, the body holds ultimate power. Here, culturally ingrained fear has turned the body into something to gain dominion over in order to maintain an illusion of control. But the reality is, at some point, our bodies will usher us into the unknown and school us. If we can shift fear into awareness and willingly follow its lead, a conscious relationship with body can initiate another level of power. Then the body as a doorway no longer leads to an avenue of control but becomes a compass to guide our healing journey.

....

EXERCISE: Contemplate your relationship with food or sexuality. How has your body already been teaching you?

....

Navigating the Unknown Body

As a teacher, body holds a key to navigating the unknown. As the medium between life and death, body contains the ultimate mystery. No matter how much information we gather to negotiate issues like health, food, weight, sexuality, and fertility, at most we're establishing a baseline for making educated guesses about self-care. What helps you may or may not work for me. Sorting through individual needs to create balance begins in relationship with the body.

I believe our fear-based culture discourages an authentic empowered relationship with body. Our either/or dualistic world overvalues the mind and objectifies the body. Notice how our educational system focuses on developing the brain with comparatively little attention given to physical education or even substantial bodily movement throughout the day. As we grow up, between sports, health care, and the media, the body becomes an object and even a commodity to control and manipulate for success. Open a magazine and see airbrushed images promising beauty, wealth, or sexual prowess through purchasing a certain jacket, vehicle, or shade of lipstick. By dividing the mind and body into separate and unequal parts, our culture systematically undermines wholeness among our mental, physical, emotional, and energetic bodies.

Women's bodies are especially objectified; I recently saw an ad of a woman's torso turned into a bottle of alcohol. In fact, when it comes to women, between rigid beauty standards and sexual mores as well as increasingly mechanized pregnancy and childbirth, our culture treats a woman's body as territory to control like the earth itself. Certainly the way many cultures across the globe continue to plunder women and the earth—from systematically raping masses of certain ethnic women to relentlessly consuming our limited natural resources—illustrates our deeply traumatized and unconscious relationship with body.

When it comes to finding meaning through pain, I turn to the Greek myth of Chiron, the wounded healer. Because of his half-horse appearance, Saturn's son, Chiron, was abandoned at birth. Chiron raised himself, becoming a great musician, astrologer, and wise teacher to heroes such as Jason, Achilles, and Hercules. One day, Hercules accidentally shot a poisoned arrow into Chiron's leg that didn't kill him (because of his immortal lineage) but produced chronic pain. This injury led Chiron to study healing herbs and potions, knowledge he then passed on to his students.

The story of Chiron demonstrates how the healing that people cultivate through their greatest pain can become their deepest source of wisdom. The levels of unprocessed trauma the body holds emotionally, physically, and energetically is what makes it such a powerful portal for healing. When unconsciousness has turned a body into a toxic waste site, cleanup will take time. But as teachers of the unknown, fear, awareness, and choice can facilitate a different kind of relationship with body.

It's possible to invite a conversation with your body that relies on listening instead of lecturing. Deciphering your body's language requires patience and commitment. As the connection deepens, trust grows. Health challenges become an opportunity to attune differently and discover meaning. In time, the body can transform into a tuning fork for self-realization.

Body is right here, right now. A conscious body leads to experiencing daily life in a whole new way. The rest of this chapter shares real-life stories of how the body initiates people into awakening consciousness. May these experiences encourage your own conscious conversation with body as a teacher.

EXERCISE: Contemplate some of your wounds. Do they relate to body? How has your body asked you to enter the unknown?

Introducing Melissa

As I began writing this chapter, my friend "Melissa" offered to reveal her story about body as a teacher. After we met I realized that, like the wounded healer Chiron, Melissa's relationship with her body illustrates how great pain transforms into wisdom.

The first twenty years of Melissa's life were spent experiencing and escaping violation. Melissa was the product of a short marriage between her sixty-one-year-old father and twenty-two-year-old mother. After her parents divorced, Melissa's mother relinquished custody and left the state. Melissa had no contact with her mother during childhood. Her aging father was well-meaning but ill-equipped to raise her, so he left his golden-haired, bright-eyed daughter in the care of untrustworthy people.

The first person to sexually abuse Melissa was a neighbor living across the street. During our visit, Melissa explained, "I witnessed this happening and watched myself closing down. I did speak to this man the next day and told him that I knew that what he had done was wrong and that he needed some help. And then I ran away from home." Melissa was seven years old. From the age of seven through eighteen, five different people sexually abused Melissa. The same instinct that propelled Melissa to run for her life at seven carried her through adolescence, when she repeatedly left behind one abuser after another in search of a safe place to call home.

By this point, life had dented Melissa. As her teenage body developed, she tried to keep people away by hiding inside bulky, unattractive clothing and bathing infrequently. "It [the abuse] closed me down so that I couldn't receive a hug or even a handshake. Just having to cross a bridge of skin touching skin was overwhelming." When Melissa did eventually begin dating later in her teens, she experienced a date rape and then stayed with the man for two years. She maintained a pattern of volatile codependent relationships with men into her twenties, when she chose being alone over perpetuating dysfunction.

EXERCISE: How are you disconnected from your body? Imagine you're meeting your body for the first time. What does it need in this moment?

Seeds of Awakening

Between the ages of eighteen and twenty-seven, Melissa's irrepressible spirit began to shine through the cracks of trauma and call her back to herself. Through a series of experiences, Melissa recovered trust.

Her awakening began at eighteen with a defining moment regarding the violating neighbor who still lived across the street from her father. She felt so much rage that, one day, she took one of her father's loaded guns and rang her neighbor's doorbell. After repeatedly ringing the bell and no one answering, Melissa sat on the porch and burst into tears. Then she had an epiphany. "I realized that even if he were dead and I got my revenge, it wouldn't take any of these feelings away. I was going to have to find another way to make myself whole again." Melissa's need to cultivate a different kind of healing birthed choice. "In that moment, I learned that we really can create our own choices just by setting an intention. And then we start to see more and more of those choices available to us."

Melissa chose to develop her intellect because she wasn't ready to engage her female body. "I was analytical. I was logical. And I could just forget about anything below the neck." She graduated college with an engineering degree and then relocated to Texas to become a chemical engineer. In Texas, Melissa started exercising and changing her diet, gradually turning vegetarian. On the outside she looked like a successful woman in her mid-twenties thriving in a male-dominated field, but being vegetarian in the land of Texas barbecue differentiated her from others.

Melissa's sense of isolation opened a line of communication between herself and her body. "I thought I had done everything right, so how could I feel so empty? I'm alone. I'm not making friends. I can't find food to nourish my body. I feel like a fish out of water. I'm going through the motions, but I'm not really here. This is where my intuition started to wake up and speak to me, very gently saying, 'There is more, and you are deeper than this. You have other needs than this. This isn't about meeting some checklist that society has generated about what you're supposed to do in this culture.'"

At this moment, synchronicity arrived as a free ticket to a weekend seminar with Anthony Robbins, a transformational self-help author and leader. Melissa came away intrigued by the possibility that people could change their state of being through engaging their physiology. When Melissa was offered free entrance into a Tony Robbins yearlong training program, she took a risk. "I decided on the spur of the moment to quit my job, sell everything I owned, and jump into the unknown. . . . Something welled up inside of me and said, 'You must forget everything you know and take a real leap of faith. This is a real moment of trust.'" After a garage sale settled her debts "to the penny," Melissa left Texas to discover new frontiers.

EXERCISE: Identify a moment when you took a leap of faith. How did synchronistic events encourage you? What did you learn?

Turning Points

Melissa spent the next year traveling the world, studying with and eventually working for Tony Robbins. She swam with dolphins, flew over volcanoes, and learned Neuro-Linguistic Programming. Letting go of security and status taught her about trust and pleasure. And yet, some lessons came from overcoming obstacles.

At one point, Melissa was invited to live with a yoga teacher and her husband and teenage daughter in Mexico. Because of her white skin, light blue eyes, and golden hair, Melissa was warned not to leave the house to avoid being targeted for rampant neighborhood kidnappings for ransom. Given her lack of family, ransom was not viable for Melissa, so a kidnapping could result in her murder. One day, the yoga teacher's husband approached Melissa and tried to seduce her. This time, Melissa held her ground. "I stood in the full power of my body and said, even with the consequence of death, 'What you have just said is completely disrespectful to me, to your daughter, to your loving wife, to yourself. . . . You can kick me out if you want, and I'm happy to go. As a matter of fact, you're taking me to the airport and I'm getting a ticket. And if I die on the streets, I'm still going to defend my body. Because my body is my body, and nothing and no one is welcome without a personal invitation from me." The husband promptly drove Melissa to the airport, and she returned to the States, where she eventually settled in New Mexico. This moment marked a turning point where Melissa left victimhood behind.

Melissa arrived in New Mexico at age twenty-seven as an awakened woman. She'd faced fear, grown awareness, and left behind codependent conflict to activate choice in her life. But body wasn't done schooling her. Melissa had sworn off romance. Then one day she met "Jeff" and felt drawn to his generosity of spirit. Raised in a loving family filled with generations of happily married people, Jeff had not suffered loss, yet he still knew compassion. He intuitively gave Melissa space; their first night together was spent holding hands without a kiss.

Gradually, Melissa and Jeff fell in love. In her past relationships with men, sex was a chore, but with Jeff, love and trust heightened attraction. Melissa needed to decide how to reveal her history of sexual abuse. "I didn't want to share this with him because I didn't want to be viewed as tainted goods. But I did share a little bit with him—just not the number, not the details of the violations." Then Melissa took another courageous step. "I said that I needed his patience. I wanted to open myself up and yet I had never done that before. I needed to go really slow and gentle. I needed to go at my own pace." Melissa was reclaiming her body and her life.

EXERCISE: Explore key moments when you've stood up for yourself, or others, in small or big ways. How did it help you? How might you find resolution inside without an outward experience? Remember, what do you need? How can you find support?

Turning Dead Ends into Doorways

When Body Initiates a Healing Journey

And so Melissa began inhabiting her body through a loving intimate relationship with Jeff. Following some years together, Jeff and Melissa became engaged in 2001. This moment could have marked an endpoint on Melissa's healing journey. Instead, Melissa's body initiated a new challenge when she stopped menstruating. After a pregnancy test came back negative, she had a series of medical exams. Then doctors diagnosed Melissa with prolactinoma, when an overproduction of the hormone prolactin grows a noncancerous tumor on the pituitary gland, interfering with other hormones like estrogen. Prolactinoma is not life threatening, but it can disrupt menses and cause infertility.

The loss of menstruation struck Melissa to the core and caused her to reevaluate her life. At first she blamed herself, imagining some wrongdoing, and then she began backpedaling from marriage to Jeff. Perhaps infertile, Melissa feared becoming a sick, broken woman. When Jeff responded with steady unconditional love, Melissa turned inward. Given the possibility she couldn't bear children, she began deconstructing traditional beliefs about what it meant to be a woman.

Melissa also investigated options for physical healing through Western medicine. When that failed, she moved on to alternative modalities like Chinese medicine. Melissa described the time from 2001 through 2003 as a shedding and rediscovering. "I was kind of like a canvas, and I was painting myself. I was becoming blank again, but I wasn't filled up yet." After Jeff and Melissa married in 2003, they moved to California, where an acupuncturist introduced Melissa to Maitri Breathwork. This led her to studying earth-based ways, including the Native American sweat lodge at the Stargate School through the Center for Sacred Studies.

In 2008, Melissa revisited Western medical treatment because she and Jeff were actively considering parenthood. During a particularly challenging reaction with side effects that included stroke and seizure, Melissa stopped taking the medicine. "Through the years, I really convinced myself that I was only going to succeed and be healed once I started my moon [menstruation]." Increasingly spiritual, she prayed to find the right doctor, medicine, and holistic modality, and though encouraging events happened, Melissa's period did not return. "Somewhere in the back of my mind, I thought I must not be doing something quite right." Melissa had reached a crossroads.

EXERCISE: Consider a time in your life when perseverance and creativity led to new horizons. Then consider another time when the same perseverance and creativity revealed a constant dead end. Compare the two without making either situation right or wrong. What did you learn from both experiences?

Letting Go Generates Healing

One day in 2009, Melissa decided to participate in a moon lodge, a sacred way for menstruating women to gather independently during a Native American sweat lodge. She set up the lodge and then asked for guidance about the next level of healing. "I don't want to say I'm giving up, but at what point do I let go and accept what is? How can I do that?" At that moment, a lizard came and stood on the top of Melissa's toe and bobbed its head. When pursued by a predator, a lizard can survive by offering its tail to be eaten. Then it can grow another tail. To Melissa, the lizard's appearance signified the presence of regenerative power. "Suddenly, I heard this voice, clear as day, that said, 'Go and close the circle with the doctor. Make an appointment and have a conversation with her. Then you'll know your next step.'"

After returning home, Melissa met with the doctor who had said if Melissa wasn't tolerating lower levels of medication, she needed to listen to her body. Then the doctor told Melissa there were no other treatment options. Melissa decided it was time to let go. "The moment I could put down my attachment to healing being in the form and only in the form of having my menstruation, I realized I had been heard by the Universe. I am supported and I am perfect just the way I am. . . . These weren't just thoughts. This was grace coming in and me feeling that it is the way it's supposed to be—and that, really, all of this has been nothing but opportunities for my own growth."

EXERCISE: Remember a time you couldn't achieve a desired outcome. Where did life lead you instead? What did you learn? Was body involved in some way?

Letting go expanded Melissa's perspective. "Our reality is not a punishment when we try with the purest intention to heal ourselves or get to some result and we're not there yet. To this day, I still have not bled, and I've tried so many different alternatives. I don't consider myself a failure now. . . . I've done nothing wrong." Releasing blame and shame helped Melissa realize that her desire to menstruate "was about feeling whole, being a complete woman" which she'd experienced. "So bleeding would just be a mental attachment."

In letting go of a specific outcome, Melissa found new avenues of fertility. "There are so many ways that Jeff and I can express the potency of being pregnant and giving birth to something that will have a legacy of its own." Melissa also received unexpected healing gifts of acceptance, appreciation, and "following instead of getting ahead of something." Most of all, Melissa has learned how to trust and honor her body. "You can talk and talk to your body, and there's a point where you need to make space to listen. Really listen." Today, Melissa experiences her body as sacred space.

Almost ten years later, Melissa's inability to menstruate has become "truly the biggest gift ever." Melissa wouldn't change a single thing. "I don't know how I could have arrived here where I am and love my body as deeply as I do without having gone through what I have. I don't know that I would have woken up any other way." Melissa spent her early years looking for a safe place to live. Today at forty-two years old, Melissa is indeed awake. No longer limited by past pain or future unknowns, Melissa's tenacious spirit is free to touch people. Recently, Jeff and Melissa purchased farmland they're nurturing for themselves and for a community. Melissa's choice to follow her body has generated a welcome home indeed.

EXERCISE: Write a letter to your body as if you had a friendship with it that ended badly. Explore how you and your body have disappointed each other. Be honest. Get angry. Then remember some good times. What have the hard times taught you? What would forgiveness look like?

PRACTICE: YOUR BODY AWAKENING

Go to your spiritual area and create sacred space. Breathe into your heart and call upon body as a teacher in your life. Ask to be shown a part of your body that needs attention. Imagine entering this part of your body. If you feel frozen or can't move, don't push but instead journal or draw your experience. Explore your surroundings. What does this part of your body need? What might you need to let go? Notice any shame, blame, and guilt. Interact with your body, remembering to ask for help.

When this feels complete, express gratitude to your body for working so hard to sustain your life. When you're ready, breathe into your heart. Open your eyes and journal, draw, dance, sing, or just be with your experience. Notice any images, sounds, sensations, colors, textures, or feelings. When you're ready, close your circle.

Note: Do not do this practice without support if you have a history of untreated trauma.

The Paper Fan

In my daily life, synchronicity has been surprising me with more lessons on the power of body to awaken consciousness. At the beginning of this chapter, I mentioned that I have several close pregnant women in my life right now. A few days ago, I traveled from San Francisco to Portland for a weekend trip to facilitate a small blessingway for a beloved thirty-eight-week-pregnant friend, Nicole. A blessingway is a spiritual gathering that honors a woman's transition to motherhood. After landing, I received a voicemail from Nicole saying her fiancé, James, was picking me up because she had been having "intense" contractions all night. "And by the way, welcome to Portland."

Upon arrival at her house, I greeted Nicole with a tight hug. I pulled away, and we stood belly to bigger belly, my brown eyes searching her green gaze. Her eyebrows raised, and she shook her head in disbelief.

I squeezed her arms and asked, "Are contractions still happening?"

She nodded and smiled in a bemused way. "I can't believe you're here."

"I can get back on a plane, you know."

She shook her head adamantly. "No, no, no. You're not going anywhere. This is perfect. It's poetic." And with that, after twenty-four years of deep friendship, we entered a new frontier of labor together.

Nicole and I had met the first week of college when a guy friend with a crush asked me to spy on her. When I saw him later, I said, "She's an artist and likes James Taylor. I can't tell you anything else because she and I are going to be good friends." Nicole and I have held each other through most big life moments: weddings, baby showers, career transitions, family drama, and deaths. Our soul-searching conversations span years. Probably lifetimes.

When I let go of my professional relationship with pregnancy and birth, including being a doula, Nicole called me three times a week for six months, becoming my safest place. As her beloved dog of eighteen years was dying in her arms, I crooned to Nicole over the phone. Sometimes we can be at cross-purposes. Whereas Nicole speeds through a store tossing groceries into a cart, I scour labels.

As my teenage children fly free, she's entering motherhood. Yet we always find a way to struggle and then laugh across any distance, coming back to claim each other no matter what.

The tricky thing about a first baby is determining whether labor is actually happening. A few hours after I arrived, Nicole's contractions measured twelve to fifteen minutes apart. I suggested she have half a glass of wine and take a bath to test if the labor was genuine, as the wine could stop contractions in a false alarm. Toward early evening as Nicole tested this theory, I received a surprise call from my midwife friend and former colleague, Hokhmah Joyallen, whom I hadn't spoken with for months.

Hokhmah said, "Hey, lovie, I had a vivid dream early this morning and had to call you. I went into [my son] Noah's room and he was really small, like a baby. Is everything okay?"

Getting chills, I said, "You're never going to guess what's happening. Do you have a moment?" With that, I was able to consult with the woman whose midwifery I most respect in the world—the woman with whom I cocreated Birthing Intuition, a holistic childbirth preparation course, and who unofficially mentored me into doulahood. As we spoke, I flashed on glistening strands of light forming a web of life, a web of birth. Hokhmah and I remained connected inside. The gift of her presence fortified me.

Suffice to say, despite the wine, by early evening Nicole's contractions intensified to six or seven minutes apart. Normally, as a woman moves further into labor, she becomes more primal, appearing flushed, talking less, and emoting more. Nicole seemed unchanged, traversing contractions like ripples on one of her whitewater kayaking trips. She'd disappear to do something, come drop on her knees and breathe so we could press her back, then she'd be up again, even laughing and making jokes. When a dear friend Sage arrived with a preordered blessingway meal of Indian food, Nicole ate vegetable samosas between dropping to the floor.

At about seven o'clock at night, I realized Nicole's labor was mirroring her vigorous approach to life. As if on cue, James, Sage, and

I spun into action toward leaving for the hospital. As I packed food, I noticed Nicole was hitting the floor at shorter intervals. Within thirty minutes, her contractions had shifted into warp speed at three minutes apart.

James drove, and I sat in the back seat with Nicole, who was on all fours, her head resting on my knee. When Nicole began to primal scream, I joined her in support. Apparently, outer Portland has a lot of tree-lined S-curved roads. I began to wonder why the fifteen-minute hospital ride was taking so long. Then we pulled into a gas station. James signaled to a doe-eyed young attendant who politely approached the car. Ignoring all four open windows, Nicole and I howled "*Aaahhhhhh!*" as the increasingly wide-eyed boy stuttered directions, looking anywhere but the back seat. The car ride to the hospital lasted forty minutes. Upon our arrival, James parked and Nicole was ushered toward the maternity ward well ahead of me. With five hospital bags strapped across my chest, I chased her down the hall, still screaming in unison to maintain contact.

Upon examination, the nurse said Nicole was nine centimeters dilated. No longer making jokes, Nicole continued to sound. She was deep in transition, the point between seven and ten centimeters just before pushing, when contractions are usually the most intense. In Birthing Intuition, Hokhmah and I correlate transition with initiation, a moment of realization. Initiation necessitates surrendering into the unknown and asks a woman to deepen faith and trust. Here, it's normal for a woman to say, "I can't do it," to want to stop the process any way she can, especially with medication. She's facing the edge of her perceived limitations and must push through resistance to discover her well of power.

Had this been a normal doula situation, I would have had a chance to discuss this moment with Nicole and James in advance. We would have role-played scenarios and made agreements about support. I knew Nicole was not vested in a natural birth, but she hadn't been adamant about drugs either. Suddenly, I heard Nicole say, "I want something. Fentanyl." The nurse said it might be too close to the baby's birth. Then Nicole said, "An epidural. I want an epidural."

With no immediate response from anyone, I stepped in. "Nicole, honey, I know this is hard, but you're almost there. You're almost at pushing. If you have an epidural, it's going to make everything longer. You don't need an epidural."

She yelled at me, *"I want an epidural, now."*

I got in her face, *"Nicole. Hear me. I'm calling upon twenty years of friendship with you. Right here. Right now. An epidural will slow everything down. You can do this. You're almost there. Trust me."* Nicole gave me her most stubborn glare. James looked angry. I softened my voice, "How about you get checked and see where you are?" Nicole agreed and thankfully, she had dilated ten centimeters.

As Nicole began pushing, I reached for the one thing I had brought from my old doula bag—an Asian-styled paper fan with pink and yellow flowers. My doula clients swore by the relief of fresh air it offered between pushes. I had planned on gifting it to Nicole at her blessingway. Now twelve hours later, Sage and I took turns gently fanning our beloved friend. Always ahead of the curve, Nicole birthed her daughter quickly. After baby Ari emerged, she rested on her mama's chest, her eyes wide open and alert. Weighing five pounds, nine ounces, Ari didn't cry at all. She recognized her mama's skin as home and remained peaceful for a long time.

After sleeping only a few hours, I woke up feeling the enormity of birth. How a conscious birthing body leads a woman through layer upon layer of resistance and release, resistance and release, until the final moments of surrender, when she merges with birth to become a doorway of life. Here, surrender rarely appears as a harp-strumming choir of angelic bliss. With body as the nexus, surrender in birth is more often an earthly shedding, challenging a woman to release everything she knows, to empty into undiluted rawness. Over and over and over again. In the releasing, she clears the way for everyone—herself, her partner, and her child—to begin a new life. In the merging, a birthing woman embodies transformation.

Yesterday, I needed to remain standing to navigate the surprise of being at my dearest friend's birth. Now on the other side of adrenaline, I fell into an ocean of feeling. I cried at the power of birth. I shook inside the vulnerability of surrender. I choked on the helplessness of letting go. The pain of fighting with Nicole washed over me. Recognizing my fear of disturbing her initiation at such a potent time, I dove underneath to the razor's edge between resistance and release and pressed further as it sliced me into pieces. I held still while birth broke me open.

From there, I followed trust. Nicole and I had not planned for me to attend her birth. I began to notice archetypal theater at play. In a delicate moment, I had trusted Nicole's capacity to face her pain. At vulnerable times in my life, Nicole has never wavered. While birth had been new territory for us, I found peace in the familiar rhythm of our constancy.

Later that day at the hospital, Sage, James, Nicole, and I compared notes. Mistakes became points of humor. Vulnerability punctuated strength. Coincidence illustrated magic. In a moment when we were alone, baby Ari on her chest, Nicole said she was both pissed off and glad I challenged her about an epidural. After twenty-four years of meeting each other head on, Nicole had not been cowed by my bigness. Choice had been with her during surrender.

Toward the end of our visit, Nicole expressed concern about handling her wedding in two months with a babe in arms, and I teased, "Hey, you just birthed a baby out of your body, you Amazon Birth Goddess. Is there anything you won't be able to manage from now on?" She shook her head with a similar bemused smile as the day before, a lifetime ago, and said, "No, I don't think anything will ever be hard again—that's coming in fast." I nudged her, "Fast? You? Impossible." Nicole laughed, and we hugged goodbye.

Since coming home, I've been pondering the blessings a woman's body offers through childbirth. If she's fortunate, the moments when a woman surrenders and merges with the power of birth leave a lasting impression on her life. A birth plan gone awry shows her how letting go is necessary to make way for change. Leaning into her partner helps her develop strength through vulnerability. Laboring through exhaustion reminds her how far she can stretch to nurture what she loves. If she's fortunate, through every hard and beautiful moment of initiation in childbirth, a woman learns to recognize herself as a source of strength and wisdom. She realizes her capacity for transformation however she expresses it in the world. And while these blessings may come through a birthing body, they arrive as gifts for us all to cherish and make our own.

PRACTICE: LOVE YOUR BODY

Go to your spiritual area with a copy of the Co-commitment Triangle, bringing a journal or drawing materials. Create sacred space. Focus on a part of your body, choosing a new part or staying with the body part that came forward during the last practice. How can you offer this part of yourself love, appreciation, and acceptance? Refer to the Co-commitment Triangle for help. Get creative—draw a picture, write a love letter, sing a song, imagine a beautiful color or picture filling this part of your body. Choose an image, color, or word from the above experience to represent love, acceptance, and appreciation. Close your circle, offering gratitude.

As you move through your daily life, bathe your body part in this one image, color, or word. Be on the lookout for resistance and barking dogs to challenge you. When they do, don't push anything away. Instead, notice any fears or other feelings that arise so you can discover what hinders your relationship with body. Drawing upon earlier practices in this book, go to your spiritual area and care for those painful parts. Meanwhile, in your daily life, continue to practice embodying love, acceptance, and appreciation.

Embodying Joy through Movement

Body as teacher wouldn't be complete without recognizing the healing power of movement through yoga, dance, surfing, martial arts, and more. Here, I'll share how my relationship with dance arrived as a lifeline out of a deep well of body pain.

By the age of fifteen, body was not my friend. Growing up amidst the shadow of my mother's potential blindness instilled distrust. As I moved deeper into my teens, friends revealed experiences of sexual abuse, further establishing body as dangerous terrain. Then weird food reactions and oddly timed tingling hands estranged me further. But what really turned my body from an unsafe acquaintance into an enemy was its size.

I wasn't born skinny, or even what you might call average. As a kid growing up in San Francisco in the seventies and eighties, I was too feminist for pink tutus but not brave enough for team sports. By the time I was thirteen, finding jeans my size took me to the deepest end of the clothing rack. Whether it's my voluptuous Jewish genes, a sedentary childhood, or a sluggish thyroid, I've always leaned toward (and sometimes past) chunky.

Don't get me wrong. Growing up inside a community of feisty, round, mostly lesbian women taught me to question cultural norms and find strength in difference. If I criticized myself, Mom pointed at my rounded belly and argued, "What, this small curve? You know what's in there? Your womb. You have a womb inside you, and it needs some space around it to be healthy." Mom herself modeled balanced eating, and she jogged for years. But ultimately, it would be on me to cultivate a healthy relationship with my body. And so, in 1984, when Mom invited me at age fifteen to attend a Rhythm & Motion dance class with her, I agreed.

Even in the midst of teenage angst, Rhythm & Motion Dance Workout Program captivated me. The hour of exercise was organized into sections by song and tempo. Each song drew from a base of choreography, creating a foundation on which to build. We arched our backs and circled our hips as we warmed up to Bill Withers' "Ain't No Sunshine." We forward-jumped and thrust pelvises to "It's Raining Men" by the Weather Girls. We crunched stomachs and lifted legs to Sade's "Your Love Is King." Learning the choreography kept our minds busy and focused while the variety of music, from world to pop beats, invited us to dance.

The professional dance teachers' warm welcome made learning dance feel like coming home. One teacher raised her arms in a graceful stretch and wrapped us in a blanket of elegant love. Another taught the nuance of each move as if we were professional dancers in training. And with a committed yet playful wave from her hips, a third teacher radiated motivation that transformed each class into a spiritual experience.

While dancing, we stared at our beautiful instructors to learn the choreography. In the early days, there were no mirrors so, dressed in my electric blue leotard, matching leg warmers, and white terry headband, I was free in the delusion that I looked good. In fact, I could fantasize that I looked *really* good, like the dancer teaching the class.

What could this mean to a fifteen-year-old chunky, sedentary girl?

Everything.

Participants in the classes were almost always women ranging from twenty to fifty years old with body sizes as varied as their ages. To move alongside adult women as they gloried in themselves normalized my experience. Eagerness permeated the air and blessed my fifteen-year-old explorations of sensual body pleasures without making me into an object for someone else's disdain or enjoyment. In the flow between inner journey and outward connection, I saw people making their own way with dance.

I carried these weekly experiences into my first high school dance. In the middle of Lowell High School's courtyard, I could lean on a Rhythm & Motion twirl while my body discovered how to translate the beat of a song into an expression of movement. Giving my hips the freedom to sway transcended teenage self-consciousness. By the time I went to college, the dance floor was a place to inhabit myself fully. Dance had taught me how to make friends with my body.

As I grew up, married, and had two children, I continued to dance. In 1995, I danced naked and pregnant in my living room the night before my daughter was born. In 2002, inspired by spiritual training with Stargate School, my dear friend Sue Lockyer and I cocreated Sacred Dance, an evening of intuitive, freestyle body movement. Our intention was to explore dance, not as a performance but as a spiritual practice—to create a safe place where movement is the medicine and there's no way to dance wrong.

Today, ten years later, Sue has moved elsewhere and I now cofacilitate private and public Sacred Dances with Jill Pettegrew. After what dance has given me, it's a privilege to help people cultivate movement as a healing path. The Rhythm & Motion Dance Workout Program continues to thrive in San Francisco under the guidance of founder Consuelo Faust. Dancing there each week helps move me through life. A tired morning shows me how to persevere. I stretch and explore possibility. My arching back welcomes sensuality. Sweat emerges as clarifying release. Leaping reminds me to take risks playfully. Through dance, I embody joy.

During a painful teenage time, dance introduced me to a natural place, inside and out, where I could be big and feel free. Today, while I'm no longer at the deepest end of the rack of jeans, I'm at peace in the double digits. Dance hasn't made me thin, but it has helped my body grow strong. Designating my dancing female body as a sacred space has gifted me with a different kind of healing in my life, healing that can't be measured on a scale but shines through as I roll my hips and I glory in the power of my curves.

EXERCISE: What helps you move through life? How can your body become a source of joy? Do one thing this week for sensual enjoyment that's also healthy for your body. Take a walk in a natural setting. Sing. Dance to a favorite song (in your home, no mirror). Try a new workout class. Ask someone to rub your feet. Soak in a bath.

Body, the Constant Teacher

As I've been writing, life continues to communicate the pervasiveness of body as a teacher. Three days ago, a heart came in for Dayna's now eight-month-old daughter, Dyllan. My first prayer was for the family who lost a baby. The second was for Dyllan. In a surgery lasting almost twelve hours, Dyllan received a heart transplant. Two days after surgery, Dyllan is alive and in a delicate state. There were some complications related to her other organs, but so far, her new heart remains strong. We wait, continue to hold our points of prayer, and wait some more.

I keep remembering my conversation with Hokhmah following the heart transplant meeting we attended six months ago. "Aren't you writing about the unknown?" inquired Hokhmah. "Here we are standing at the edge of the abyss around this beautiful baby, looking into the unknown of life and death. Isn't this as deep as it gets?" I can't imagine facing a deeper, more terrifying unknown. And what makes body an ultimate doorway is that it holds the potential for both life and death. We can never know where we'll land between heaven and earth.

The other day, my husband, Alex, and I discussed what body might be communicating through Melissa, Nicole, myself, and now Dyllan. In his usual direct way, Alex said, "That's easy. The body holds, transforms, and releases. That's what these lives are showing." I would add that the force that propels people through holding, transforming, and releasing is the dance between fear and surrender. As the literal portal between life and death, body *is* a threshold for change. To manage our fear of death, our culture has turned body into an object of denial and control. But at some point, everyone faces mortality. And what is death but a kind of letting go, a surrender?

Here's where body can become a master teacher. As the threshold between life and death, body initiates us through surrender.

Initiation can be uncomfortably hot, a blazing trail of fire. A sick, traumatized, or malfunctioning body shatters denial and illusions of control, catapulting us into the unknown. Suppressed fear rises to demand our attention. I've mentioned that the size and scope of the fear we meet on the threshold of change is equal (or more) to the healing waiting on the other side. If we can surrender into following body, it will initiate us into another level of healing.

This healing can happen at any point along the way and often never ends. People with cancer, prolactinoma, or a heart defect may or may not arrive at a certain physical outcome, but they can experience a different kind of healing. A laboring woman can give life to a baby while birthing herself as a mother. Dance can be a beautiful performance and a joyful healing practice. In fact, with its ability to regenerate, body encompasses an *And* existence. Thus, a conscious relationship with body can initiate healing every day—right here, right now. Through body, daily life becomes our healing center. Here, a conscious relationship with body involves listening. A central key to learning how to listen to the body comes through developing intuition.

BODY GUIDELINES, YOUR INTEGRATIVE QUESTIONS

- How has body been a source of transformation in your life?

- How can fear regarding bodily issues (health, food, etc.) facilitate awareness and choice?

- What do you need to release, forgive, and transform to reclaim your body for yourself? Making peace with your body requires practice. Talk therapy, energy work, and expressive arts (dancing, singing, writing, drawing, sculpting, creating a ceremony) can help.

- What lessons, qualities, and healing gifts has your body initiated in your life?

- What life lessons has your body been trying to teach you through your book intention?

7

Intuition: Your Inner Compass and Fear Filter

Often in the middle of an extended group healing session, there's a point when everyone gets sleepy. A teacher once told me that underneath slouching shoulders and heavy-lidded eyes something unconscious is moving through the room. From then on, whenever a group seems to enter that time of exhaustion, I perk up. If sleepy energy means that things are just about to get interesting, I don't want to miss what might happen next.

As we pass the halfway point in making friends with the unknown, I can feel that tiredness here now. I understand the need to take a rest after journeying so far. In the middle of the birth I just attended, after pressing her head to the floor and breathing through a contraction, Nicole looked up and said, "Now I know why they call this labor." Birthing consciousness takes work too.

If you've learned just one thing from interacting with the first four teachers, you're doing well. I hope you find comfort in realizing how far you've traveled.

Let's cultivate a gentle moment to integrate where we've been. The first four teachers might dress differently, but overall their presence in daily life is apparent. Fear consistently attempts to dominate with dramatic flair and can be a red flag of attention. Awareness may come in a flash of insight, or it may take time to develop, but its arrival shakes core foundations and catalyzes change. Bodily experiences such as a simple cold, chronic illness, or childbirth naturally challenge daily routines. Lessons learned through fear, awareness, and body culminate with a conscious choice to move forward in a specific direction. While practicing conscious relationship is a subtle introspective art, engaging any of these teachers can shift the trajectory of daily life.

EXERCISE: Consider the last week or so in your life. How is fear trying to get your attention? What core beliefs are you noticing? What does conscious choice look like throughout your day? How is your body constantly teaching you?

The next four teachers—intuition, energy, intention, and surrender—expand the scope of the unknown to include a larger metaphysical world. And yet this is Practical Spirituality. I'm not asking you to believe in God to cultivate intuition. But it is important to consider what mediums help you experience meaning.

For example, while my mother is an atheist whose truest religion is *Star Trek*, many a morning when I was a child and we were eating scrambled eggs, she would ask me what I'd dreamed. Eventually, I learned my mom paid attention to dreams with numbers or animals. She'd say, "It was one of *those* dreams." This was code for the kind of dream that contained a message. Today, I have a vivid dream life, probably because of those scrambled egg conversations. What earmarks *those* dreams is when they arrive with a whoosh of underlying sensation. Whether we believe a message is from God, Goddess, Spirit, our psyche, or the collective unconscious, it's our intuition—our internal compass and lifeline of trust—that helps us sort through the static and take action as we feel our way through the unknown.

PRACTICE: GROUND YOURSELF—
REFINING THE POINT OF AN ARROW

Let's fortify your intention by revisiting a few points. Some intentions inspire months of learning, while others are fleeting. Following an intention can be like peeling layers of an onion to discover core meaning. Or an intention can be an unending spiral where each turn reveals more about what we're learning.

Wherever you are with intention, create a sacred circle and ground yourself. Consider how fear, awareness, choice, and body have informed your intention. Then reflect on what you need right now. If your current intention feels strong, like a firm shoe that can support you in traveling further, then stay with it. If your intention feels floppy, too stretchy to take a step, then refine it. Don't abandon your original intention, simply hone it to reflect what you've learned so far.

Intuition as an Inner Compass

There isn't really a singular definition of intuition. What people believe they're tapping in to through intuition varies. Some sources consider intuition to be a form of listening, a sixth sense, or a multi-sensory perception. Others experience it as a gut feeling, an instinctive inner knowing. At its core, intuition relates to a sense of perception that we can focus inward or outward to expand learning. Perception often leads people to a belief about reality.

And here's where intuition can get tricky. Because intuition is a representative of wisdom, people can throw expectations onto it. Intuition receives pressure to be right. How can we follow intuition if it isn't correct? Can you imagine where this kind of thinking might take intuition? Straight into a dualistic either/or view of reality where conflict governs. And what happens to intuition's sense of perception when it becomes caged inside roles of Victim, Persecutor, and Rescuer? Not much. Intuition is muffled.

The same desire for correct answers can lead to the commoditization of intuition. Developing intuition then becomes a method of control—a technique—to achieve a desired outcome. Intuition is perceived as an invisible key to success. From this perspective, acquiring intuition can seem shiny and glamorous. Behind the mystique, we're just looking for a way to manage fear inside the reality of not knowing.

I'd like to release the belief that intuition needs to be correct in order to grow a relationship with it. Whether your intuition is right or wrong is beside the point. Instead, focus on how your intuition—not your neighbor's intuition, not your guru's intuition, not your best friend's intuition—might communicate with you. Don't worry about accuracy just yet. (You'll revisit accuracy later after you and your intuition have gotten to know each other.) Instead, practice noticing what you perceive so it has room to grow without turning it into a singular objective reality. That's the *And* atmosphere that intuition needs to thrive.

I'll share a secret. I've spent years sitting across from people who want to develop intuition to feel happier. I want that for them too. And I've noticed that developing intuition is code for something else, something deeper than control. Inside a need for intuition lives a yearning to learn how to trust—oneself, emotions, decisions, other people, relationships, the unknown. And guess what? Intuition and trust go hand in hand. Accessing intuition is a practice of learning how to trust. The more you trust, the further your perception will expand. The further your sense of perception expands, the more you'll learn how to trust. What might life inside the unknown mean if intuition and trust were in your back pocket? Or better yet, embodied in your heart and belly?

In this way, intuition becomes an inner compass. Intuition helps magnify significant sensations regarding inner and outer world experiences. Intuition can be the hair at the nape of your neck standing at attention when someone walks too closely behind you. Or when you get the chills after someone says something wise. Intuition can be flashing on a friend's name and then picking up the phone to hear her voice on the line. Intuition is also that urge to phone someone who then answers saying, "Wow, I was just about to call you."

Intuition also helps you decipher how you feel about inner and outer world experiences. It's an inner voice or urge telling you to take a different road today, accept that new job, or even let go of a dream. In this way, intuition is a tool to sort through beliefs, feelings, and experiences to generate meaning. You learn to pay attention when you get the chills, because someone (including you!) might be saying something wise. Perhaps this wise advice might inspire you to take that job or let go of a dream. From there, trust fosters choice and movement. Connecting, receiving, and sorting through inner or outer sensory information can make a big difference in navigating daily unknowns.

EXERCISE: Contemplate your own sense of intuition. Have you ever noticed a physical sensation, an image, an urge, or a word that informed an experience in your everyday life? If not, ask some wise people in your life about intuition. Consider their answers, not to be like them but to inspire a conversation within yourself.

Let's Get It Started: Accessing Intuition

A central issue is how to access intuition. Here, I need to claim my bias: I believe that intuition exists and we don't need to develop it. What we're developing is a relationship with it. The question is how to turn up intuition's volume and decipher communication. The challenge is that unresolved pain and overactive mental energy also exist, and they generate static that interferes with reception. Thus accessing intuition involves clearing the way for it to fully inhabit our being.

While intuition exists for everyone, some people seem to access it more easily than others. I don't know why. Certainly, mainstream culture doesn't emphasize intuition. Perhaps especially intuitive people just have less static. There may also be a genetic component. Whether intuition comes easily or not, I've seen enough "regular" people develop a relationship with intuition that I trust it's possible for you. Just remember we're not going for professional-grade intuition here. This isn't about hanging out a shingle as a psychic. The value of accessing intuition doesn't come through predicting a certain outcome but in discovering healing gifts along the way. This is *your* intuition. And your intuition has a talent for greeting you with creative lessons especially designed to foster growth.

When I sit with individuals and groups, I hold sacred space for people to excavate unresolved pain through personal reflection. I also offer a variety of experiential practices like guided visualization, energy work, Sacred Dance, and Maitri Breathwork. Entering these non-ordinary states of consciousness invites intuition to come forward and lead the way. My role is to facilitate these processes but also to help notice how individuals are accessing intuition. Like spiritual detectives, we look for clues about potential contact with intuition. Over time, trust and relationship grow.

Last night when Alex and I were discussing intuition, he said, "Going directly into intuition is difficult. Some things require a soft focus to learn." I've offered short practices in this book to help soften your focus, and there is also a grounding guided visualization on my website. The rest of this chapter draws upon the five senses in relation with awareness, body, and fear to help you notice how you access intuition. I invite you to put on your spiritual detective hat and investigate intuition in your daily life. From there, we'll discover how elements converge to locate intuition as an inner compass of wisdom.

EXERCISE: Do you have a very strong mind? Active anxiety? What belief systems do you have about intuition? Beyond right or wrong, assess your current relationship with intuition as if it were a potential life partner.

The Five Senses and Intuition

Some people believe that because intuition is a sixth sense, an extra or multisensory perception, it is by definition beyond the five senses. From an *And* perspective, just because intuition may be the sixth sense doesn't separate it from the other five. Over the past fifteen years, I've consistently witnessed people grow a relationship with their intuition through the five senses. If intuition involves accessing an expanded realm of perception, the five senses help unlock the door, and in some cases, act as the doorway itself.

To illustrate how people access intuition through their five senses, let's revisit some examples from previous chapters. In body as teacher, Melissa consistently experienced her intuition as an inner voice. She began noticing dissatisfaction with her life in Texas. "My intuition started to wake up and speak to me, very gently saying, 'There is more, and you are deeper than this. You have other needs than this. This isn't about meeting some checklist that society has generated about what you're supposed to do in this culture.'" In fact, a voice urged Melissa to leave engineering. "Something welled up inside of me that said, 'You must forget everything you know and take a real leap of faith. This is a real moment of trust.'" Years later she asked for guidance about her health. "Suddenly, I heard this voice, clear as day, that said, 'Go and close the circle with the doctor. Make an appointment and have a conversation with her. Then you'll know your next step.'" At pivotal moments, Melissa experienced intuition through auditory messages.

Melissa's relationship with sound shows up in other areas of her life too. She sings, plays several musical instruments, and has spent years studying sound healing. It's no coincidence that she connects with intuition through an auditory channel. While I'm no professional musician, I've studied world music for over ten years, weaving together musical journeys for a variety of groups. Often my intuition communicates with me through a song. In fact, the song that came with this intuition chapter is "Let's Get It Started" by Black Eyed

Peas. The next time a song randomly appears, you might enjoy listening to what it has to say.

EXERCISE: Creativity and intuition are related. Do you love music? Visual art? Dance? Physical activity? Are you tactile? Sensitive to smell? Do you feel deeply?

A large number of people connect with intuition through vision. This makes sense, given our cultural emphasis on the visual in daily life. It's one reason most people can readily access guided visualization. In the fear chapter, Diana experienced an image of a dragon peeling away to reveal a little girl. For months, Diana's vision connected her with a little girl as a source of intuition and healing. In the chapter on awareness, during a challenging medical procedure, Phoebe saw an image of a golden gossamer blanket of protection. Imagining the blanket surrounding her empowered Phoebe. She also received instruction (hearing) and used her breath (body sensation) to rely on her intuition to guide her through a difficult moment.

I'd like to highlight color within the realm of vision. Like sound, color can be its own medium of healing. Color inspires intuition. In our visual world, color is everywhere and completely accessible. We can consciously choose colors to wear, draw, or call upon with inner vision. In the awareness chapter, color emerged to help Tina navigate her anxiety. As she moved into her heart, vibrant yellow and compassionate pink helped her sort through thin black lines of mean thoughts. She then brought the power of color into her daily life by painting her new apartment.

A strong relationship with touch, taste, sight, smell, and sound will help you access your intuition. In fact, you can notice which of your senses stand out. In connecting intuition with a specific sense, I've noticed that intuition flashes several times: toward the beginning of a big life moment and afterward when you're reviewing or remembering in hindsight. When you're first learning, it's normal to miss intuition flashing during a big life moment. But you can pay attention to your senses as you look back and remember an experience. Perhaps a whisper of perception arrived through the airwaves. Or a voice echoed a sentence inside. A random image appeared. Or maybe your heart or belly constricted with an emotion.

I often review life moments and experiential practices with people to notice which of the five senses appeared. Was it in the form of a word, sensation, image, feeling, smell, taste, dream, color, or sound? Noticing what arrived this second time around in hindsight provides information about each person's specific intuition. Over time, it's possible to identify a couple of senses to follow closely in order to heighten intuition. And while you can access intuition in many ways, focusing on one or two senses is a helpful beginning. Here, awareness can shed light on what's been inside you all along.

PRACTICE: NOTICING YOUR SENSES

Go to your spiritual area and create sacred space. Journal a pivotal life moment, and while writing, list any senses that helped you perceive meaning (you can also pay attention to what senses arrive as you're journaling and write those down). How did you realize you were in love for the first time? What inspired you to accept a life-changing job? Or take a leap of faith with a bold decision? Then review what you've written and notice a couple of senses—hearing, vision, colors, body sensations—that seemed to draw more attention during that key moment in your life. When you're ready, express gratitude and close your circle.

Next, begin to notice what senses appear in daily life to help you find meaning regarding events, decisions, and relationships. Follow creative pursuits—someone who loves art may be more visual, a music lover more auditory, and a dancer more drawn to body-based sensation. Is there a correlation between the senses you notice within yourself and daily life?

The Art of Noticing Your Senses

I've consistently invited you to notice images, sounds, sensations, color, texture, feelings, and more through practices, exercises, and daily life happenings. What this means is that you've been cultivating sensory perception throughout this book. Surprise! This is where you reap the benefits of showing up for yourself. Whether you've been journaling, visualizing, or studying life, my intention has been to help you grow your relationship. Drawing upon that material now can help identify your naturally stronger senses. If you haven't been able to do this, trust your pace. It's never too late to begin again.

To become more aware of sensation, remember the practice of noticing. Be curious. Play. Wonder. Notice what senses seem like a natural part of your life already. Consciousness often involves shining a light on something just past the edge of awareness. When you shift and encounter some unexplored part of yourself, something clicks into place that feels like coming home.

Notice how the swishing water of an evening bath allows your truest feelings to surface. Explore journaling as a way you might be receiving guidance. Watch a natural setting come alive behind closed eyes to reveal soulful lessons. Noticing your senses heightens intuition. Noticing is an intuitive practice unto itself.

It's no accident that the above examples involve moving inward, softening your focus, and entering a non-ordinary state of consciousness. That soft focus can come through yoga, dance, breathwork, pregnancy, guided visualization, or contemplating your nose hair. As long as you're holding an intention for conscious awareness, a soft focus can happen in many ways. At the same time, learning how to notice intuition requires some form of conscious stillness. It's possible to be physically active and simultaneously access stillness to notice, but it takes more focus.

While encouraging a sense of perception, remember that your mental body can override intuition. Mainstream culture overdevelops the mind. Maggi described how to approach the mind: "It's not about making the mind wrong; it's about helping it come into integration with the larger intelligence that even it holds. And if we can do that, then the mind becomes a beautiful tool rather than a loose cannon. But most people walk around with their mind as a loose cannon." The practice of noticing can give your mind a job so it can feel productive without necessarily taking over. Also, gently bringing your mind back to the present moment when it jumps ahead—usually with a fear—retrains it. Here, inviting your mind to notice sensory perception not only creates balance but also teaches your mind how to stay on track.

If you have journaled practices, take a moment to review some of them (as an example, see the previous practice). You can also visit my website, *www.dancing-tree.com/book,* for an audio grounding visualization. As you review, notice the ways you tend to perceive hearing, smell, touch, taste, sight, feelings, and a felt sense: Do you see images? Do you hear words? Does your body vibrate? Do colors appear? Do you feel instinctive urgings? Converging senses (for example, vision + touch + hearing) indicate intuition. An urging or instinct with a vibration that conveys a sense of knowing is intuition.

At this point, identify at least one or two senses you naturally gravitate toward. Each sense is a thread of intuition inside the unknown. Focusing on a sense will help the thread thicken into a pathway of connection. Commit to following one or two senses closely through inward practices and daily life moments.

Sitting with and Holding a Focus Awakens Body Awareness

Recognizing natural perception can be exciting and daunting. At the beginning of my apprenticeship more than fifteen years ago with Oneisha Healing Tools, a store offering products and services to help people develop awareness, journaling daily and practicing visualization amplified my auditory and visual perception. Feeling overwhelmed by the loud volume, I often complained to my teachers,

"But how do I know if this is my mind chattering or intuition that I need to follow?" Maggi or Meenakshi always answered, "Just sit with it." And so, like a hen on her egg, I started sitting with everything that arrived. Sitting with something is an active form of inner contemplation. Unlike meditating to cultivate stillness, sitting with something involves holding a focus as you engage with daily life to generate meaning.

For example, as I sat with the question of mind chatter versus intuition, everyday interactions helped me study differences. I'd have an inspirational conversation with someone. Afterward, I'd notice internal responses. Mind chatter about the interaction tended to flitter around the outside of my head, darting and piercing to escape focused attention. The texture of this kind of thought felt flimsy; breathing into mind chatter dissipated it. On the other hand, thoughts related to intuition felt more substantial. They naturally gravitated down into my belly or heart, where they seemed to take root, often stretching me in uncomfortable ways. After germinating for a period of time, lessons sprouted. Wisdom would rise up to inform an experience or situation. An endpoint arrived when my belly or heart felt spacious yet somehow more even and peaceful. Complete. From there, I would usually act on what I learned by making a decision or clarifying a relationship.

Obviously, I didn't go through this process for every conversation in the course of a day, just the ones that inspired me (sometimes because they wouldn't leave me alone!). After a while, my body developed a felt sense of the difference between mind chatter and intuition. Today, this not only helps me differentiate the two but also shows me where my mind and intuition converge to facilitate meaning.

You can hold a focus and sit with anything to develop meaning: a feeling, decision, relationship, dream, question, or more. You can sit with a decision about what to make for dinner or about whether to marry. You can sit with a specific fear or the overall issue of fear in your life. Sitting with and holding a focus can take a day or a month, or it can become a lifetime study. And while it's an inward contemplation, what's happening in your daily life informs your process. You've been sitting with an intention throughout this book. It's an inward process, but you're inviting daily life to come help you through synchronicity. Sitting with and holding a focus helps develop a conversation between your inner world, your daily life, and the unknown.

Today, "I need to sit with . . ." "I'm holding space for . . ." and "I'm studying . . ." are common phrases in my world. Sitting with something is kind of like the Slow Food Movement—the process can take more time but cultivates a sustainable way of life. Holding often includes embracing distinct points so friction can develop meaning. We've seen how my friend Shira with cancer is holding both allopathic and holistic medicine to generate healing. The process of sitting with and holding something is a practice of accessing intuition.

How you sit and hold a focus depends on what works for you. I often go back to the hen with her egg. Sitting on an egg may not look like much, but it takes quite a lot of energy to hold still while new life forms. Anyone can tap in to the energy of gestation through sitting and holding focus on a project, decision, or relationship. By practicing sitting with something meaningful in your life, you'll find your own way.

Ultimately, sitting with and holding is an energetic experience in the body. For example, you engage your intention by breathing it into your heart. Through sitting with and holding a focus, your body can transform into a conscious sorting tool. Melissa said, "The body is 100 percent truthful if we listen. It doesn't know how to lie. . . . Those habits are taught, they're not inherent in our natural programming." That's why the excavation process is so important. Releasing old beliefs, trauma, and stuck energy clears away static. Facing demons and dragons will turn your body into a tuning fork for guidance—an inner compass. A conscious body is intuition incarnate.

So as you begin to notice sensations, sit with them. What happens when you practice holding an image or color or sentence?

Where does it naturally like to land in your body? How do you experience mind chatter? How can you differentiate the mind from your intuition? Your body has its own unique way of processing incoming perceptions.

Remember that the sensations you're sitting with and holding are not random. Whether perceptions arrive through practices or everyday moments, these threads come in response to your call for conscious awakening. Engaging your body to discern creative intelligence helps transform a thread of sensation into an intuitive pathway for navigating the unknown.

EXERCISE: Journal or contemplate your relationship with your intention. What image, word, color, sensation, or feeling comes up most often? Choose one sense to sit with and hold in relationship with your intention. Where in your body does this sense gravitate toward? Notice what happens inside and throughout daily life as these energies interact.

Intuition and Fear Filter Wisdom Together

Lately when people notice their fear around me, I've responded, "Great! You must really be on to something. Keep going." Fear is a normal part of healthy development. In fact, the amount of fear that appears is often related to the potential for growth. And while I don't mean to minimize how immobilizing fear of fear (anxiety) can be, there is an essential ally that can help navigate any form of fear: intuition.

Part of what makes fear so tricky is that it can be an emotion and also a mental state. How do we know when fear is noticing a threat or trying to keep us safe yet small? When is fear an intuition, and when is fear a mental trap? For our purposes, I'm not addressing fear as an immediate physical danger, as events will reveal true threats quickly. Instead, I'm focusing on daily life fears regarding issues like health, decisions, and relationships.

For example, "Mary" has been working at a corporate office for nine years. She has dreams of starting her own business, but she just can't take the leap. Mary's concerned about finances and nervous about self-employment. But what's really keeping her awake at night is the worry that no one will think her idea is any good.

"Olivia" has lived with a kind man for seven years who supports her financially but offers little sexual intimacy. She's thirty-nine, longs to be a mother, and struggles to find work as an artist. Despite the challenges, this man is family and willing to become a father, in theory. Olivia can't decide whether to leave or stay.

Finally, "Lisa" is a healthy single mother of a six-year-old girl. Her older sister recently died of breast cancer at forty-six. Lisa just turned forty-three, and her doctor wants her to take an experimental genetic test. For Lisa, considering the test raises questions about the future and stirs up her unresolved emotions regarding her mother, who also died of breast cancer when Lisa was eight years old.

Can you see where fear might have a field day with these life circumstances? In most situations, fear is the bull in the china shop. This makes fear a great source of awareness. But how do you filter through fear to make decisions? Sitting with and holding a fear as you move through daily life can peel away layers to reveal core truths.

For example, inside Mary's dream of starting her own business is a fear that she isn't of value. As she sits with this fear, she notices a clenching in her stomach. During some inner work, Mary connects stomach clenching with not trusting herself. As she grapples with a potential business, Mary's stomach tensing and relaxing becomes a barometer for developing trust—and the strength that comes with it. Olivia has been shutting down parts of herself to maintain an unhealthy status quo. As she sits with her fear of loss through grieving her partner and her dream of having children, her heart (and pelvis!) opens. Six months later, after ending her relationship, Olivia is exploring new dating and career opportunities. Lisa's familial losses, challenging medical history, and single parenting indicate how the unknown can be quite a force of initiation. Over time, Lisa learns that acknowledging fear leads to listening to her heart and solar plexus differently, facilitating choice regarding how she holds health in her life.

Accessing intuition comes through practice. Through sitting with and holding many fears inside your body, you can begin to feel the difference between a source of intuition and a false alarm. This includes other feeling states, like joy or bliss, which can also confuse intuition. The next time you begin to fall in love, instead of rushing forward, pause for a moment to receive intuition.

Deep listening cultivates a part of you that can tell the difference between potential meaning and a force for distraction. You may know it because a strong image keeps returning. A voice urges. Your stomach tightens or relaxes. A texture feels flimsy. A special color arrives. Or a song flashes. Over time you'll be able to identify your intuition. Then when a fear makes contact, and it will, intuition can act as a counterpoint of support. While a fear is prancing around issuing grand statements of utter defeat, you can call upon intuition to help assess the situation. You can appreciate the issues that fear is flagging without buying into its dramatic flair.

Through a practice of accessing intuition, a relationship develops. Trust emerges. In an *And* world, intuition can become as strong as fear. In fact, intuition can grow strong enough to sift through static to discover the heart of fear. And when fear becomes a way to access intuition and develop wisdom, well, that's when fear becomes a true friend.

PRACTICE: EMBODYING FEAR REGARDING YOUR INTENTION

Go to your spiritual area and create sacred space. Find the drawing with your intention and different fears floating around it. After reexamining the page, identify a root fear or belief (like dented trust or self-worth). Sit with and hold this fear or belief. Where does it gravitate toward in your body? What senses arise? Play with moving the fear around to different parts of your body to see what happens. When you're ready, offer gratitude and close your circle.

Continue to sit with and hold this fear/belief in your body through everyday living. Notice how this core issue interacts with your intention. How does it keep you safe and small? How can your body and intuition help you grow wisdom? You may need help to work through these issues—make sure you seek gentle, caring support.

At the Intersection of Fear, Intuition, and Trust

While balancing group and individual sessions, I've been on call to serve as a doula for a dear friend's first birth. I gave "Lynn" and "Derrick" a doula gift certificate seven years ago as part of a wedding present. Toward the end of Lynn's pregnancy, when my mother told me that she'd had one of *those* dreams where she flashed on the number thirty with regard to Lynn's birth, I took note. Sure enough, that month on the evening of the thirtieth, a text from Derrick announced that labor had begun.

At two a.m., I entered Lynn and Derrick's home for what would become a forty-hour birth marathon. Completely dedicated to natural childbirth, Lynn experienced contractions the whole time without twenty minutes of concentrated relief. After thirty hours of labor, Lynn arrived at the hospital to learn she was just three centimeters dilated. She and Derrick rallied through disappointment and with support from a labor tub, Lynn rested awhile.

By late afternoon, the hospital urged Lynn "to get things going." When walking didn't change contractions, the hospital asked Lynn to consider other measures or receive morphine for sleep therapy. While making a decision, Lynn and Derrick discovered their baby was in a breech position. Although Lynn's regular prenatal care had indicated their baby boy was head down, the hospital doctor said he had been breech for a while. After absorbing this shock, the parents birthed their eight-pound, two-ounce son, "Asa," via cesarean.

Days passed as the new parents adjusted to infant care. One week after Asa was born, I arrived at Lynn and Derrick's home for a dinner visit. As Derrick held the baby and we set the table, Lynn remarked, "It's strange. I couldn't visualize myself giving birth. Maybe some part of me knew." Lynn had said this to me at the hospital just after learning her son was breech. She mentioned it again a couple days later during a phone call. So much had been happening that I had deflected the statements. Now seemed like a good time to respond.

I put down the plates and said, "You've told me three times in the past week that not being able to visualize giving birth feels meaningful to you."

Lynn placed napkins under forks. "Even a month ago when you asked about our vision of birth, I tried to imagine it and I couldn't see anything. I thought it was just that I needed to let go of any agenda. And so my intention was to trust what was happening no matter what. But normally, I can visualize. Now I feel like I couldn't see because it wasn't going to happen that way."

I said, "So before we learned about the breech when the hospital wanted you to get things going and you realized you were resisting contractions, that wasn't fear?"

"I was scared and I needed to learn how to relax into the contractions, but I don't think it was fear that was getting in my way. I voiced concerns that made sense, given everything, but I wasn't caught in fear. Some part of me just knew that my body wouldn't give birth naturally. That was my intuition."

"Wow, so fear was actually intuition. I'm surprised."

Lynn said, "And you know what? I'm glad I didn't know about the breech. I don't regret any of it. It is what it is, you know, Stace?"

"Yes, it is what it is. And what was your ultimate intention? To trust no matter what, yes, honey?"

Lynn said, "Yes, to trust and let go of the rest." With that, Asa fell asleep, allowing his parents a rare opportunity to enjoy a meal together.

Turning Dead Ends into Doorways

Trusting Intuition to Follow Choice

Last week, Shira called me for the first time in a while. While mothering her eight-month- and three-year-old sons full time, she'd endured more than three months of chemotherapy. Shira attributed her minimal reaction to chemo to supplemental acupuncture, herbs, vitamins, and dietary restrictions. But now Shira had reached the point of choice regarding radiation treatment.

She'd worked with a range of allopathic and holistic care providers. She'd unearthed deep emotions, tracking daytime visions and nighttime messages. When I asked about a care provider she hadn't mentioned, Shira said, "I decided not to go there. I really trust what I'm getting from all these other sources. I mean, when do I have enough information? At some point, I need to follow my intuition and trust myself. Right?"

Yesterday in an email, Shira told me she's forgoing radiation. Though her oncologist was supportive, she was his first patient to ever refuse radiation. Shira wrote, "I wish that cancer did not equal dread and fear in our culture. I wish that oncologists' offices were places that made patients feel relaxed, safe, and empowered—places where they could listen to their bodies and intuition, along with the statistics." Until this day arrives, it's up to Shira to embody an *And* world where fear and intuition meet to generate empowered decisions in her life.

As I contemplate how Lynn and Shira inform intuition, I come full circle about the issue of accuracy. While it's worthwhile to practice accessing intuition, at some point we need to be able to rely on it. Because when we're navigating a forty-hour labor or cancer treatment, intuition is not an academic exercise but a potentially precious resource. Here, it's important to reflect on how much capacity an individual's intuition can hold.

If navigating life means feeling your way through the dark, intuition is an inner compass that impacts your sense of direction. And so when the stakes are high, the practical woman in me urges you to be kind, but honest, with yourself. As a wise person, you can acknowledge growth while recognizing the limits of your capacity under stress. You can also realize when and whom to ask for help.

At the same time, you can appreciate that the ultimate gift of consciously navigating a life challenge is developing trust. You can hold the value of a positive end result alongside your ability to trust yourself no matter what. Because inside a constantly changing life, what happens next is really out of everyone's control. My vote is to do the best you can and then let the rest go.

I realize this is much easier to write about than to practice in real life, especially when the stakes are high. I'm reminded of my friend Dayna whose daughter, Dyllan, is now six weeks past a heart transplant. I can't imagine how Dayna is holding this experience, but I trust that her best is damn good. Maybe letting go makes room for trust to help hold us—and even heal us—in a different way. We can look to Lynn's intention of letting go to illustrate how trust can facilitate healing through unforeseen events. After all, who are we to demand or predict what healing should look like?

You cannot control the unknown, but you can be with the paradox. Trusting your intuition means embracing the right to be wrong. Identifying which of the five senses you naturally gravitate toward fosters relationship with a sixth sense. Sitting with and holding a focus through following senses inside your body becomes a practice of accessing intuition. Growing familiarity with your unique texture, color, image, sound, or experience of intuition facilitates relationship and furthers trust.

Even though there are no guarantees, intuition offers an edge on navigating the unknown. As an inner compass that can sort through anything—emotions, thoughts, and experiences—intuition helps you feel your way through the dark. While you work to realize dreams, ultimately your intuition cannot guarantee a particular destination. Instead, trust and intuition forge a relationship that helps you navigate the energy of life. Here, your intuition can guide you in following the energy of life to discover a path of meaning step by step along the way.

INTUITION GUIDELINES, YOUR INTEGRATIVE QUESTIONS

- What does intuition mean to you? What is your current relationship with intuition like?

- Which two senses do you naturally rely upon? Follow creative inclinations.

- How does your body sit with and hold a focus? How does it sort through daily information?

- How can your fear and intuition join forces to develop wisdom?

- If you trusted more, what would you do differently? What's one small way your trust has grown?

- Are you remembering to hold and sit with your intention daily?

8

Energy: The Heart of Navigating the Unknown

After putting herself through graduate school in psychology, forty-two-year-old "Violet" took a job as an administrative assistant to pay the bills. Two years passed until one day, Violet realized she'd forgotten her dream of becoming a psychologist. She began considering how to balance financial need with necessary licensing requirements. And things started moving. Friends approached Violet offering her a place to live at a discounted rate. Her office combined jobs, giving her an option to work more flexible hours. Violet updated her resume. A conversation produced leads for training in her intended field. From there, Violet decreased her office hours to follow the energy of her dream in daily life.

Following and navigating energy inside ourselves and through daily life touches the heart of this book. You could even say it's the point. Energy epitomizes paradox. On the one hand, energy is a spark that contains its own life force. Energy is everywhere inside everything. On the other hand, navigating energy involves noticing fear, cultivating awareness, remembering choice, embodying ourselves, and sensing intuition. Energy's essence alongside its capacity to hold some rollicking teachers translates into potent wisdom. You could say energy is a whole-enchilada teacher.

So as we enter the heart of learning, I'm grateful and excited. I'm grateful for your continued presence as I recognize your time is valuable. And I'm excited to engage in another level of conversation regarding navigating energy.

PRACTICE: GROUND YOURSELF

Create sacred space and ground yourself. As you do, welcome the teacher of energy into your life. Invite energy to inform your intention. Begin to notice your experience of energy. Because energy has been with us all along, don't be surprised if it feels familiar to you.

Energy Within and Throughout Daily Life

Part of becoming conscious involves paying attention to energy. Moving inward to study fears, question beliefs, and excavate painful experiences awakens people. Developing consciousness within everyday decisions and relationships heightens awareness further. As we realize that energy reflects all levels of relationship within and around us, energy begins to matter. This is not the kind of scientific energy my middle school–age son studies quantifying force in relationship with potential work output. This is a kind of metaphysical energy expressing universal life force that moves through everything, including the physical body. A spiritual subtle energy that people can't always see with their eyes but that nonetheless feels alive.

One way energy becomes real is through the body. Body and energy connect as a vital unit; energy helps bring a body to life. Just as the physical body can remember, layers of subtle energy fields throughout the body may also hold memory. Experiences—especially trauma—carry energetic imprints that can impact the physical and subtle bodies. Moving inward to explore feelings, beliefs, and experiences will naturally awaken the subtle energy body.

Just as inner dimensions can express life force, energy can become apparent in the context of daily life. Certainly, all sentient beings contain an essential spark, but energy also comes alive in relationship. This means that any kind of relationship reflects energy. A relationship with your best friend, sister, lover, coworker, or pet can express energy. Groups, decisions, and projects can also mirror energy. And so you can learn how to follow energy through any relationship in daily life.

In a healthier world, schools would integrate the natural intelligence of subtle energy into learning. A relationship with energy would be a normal part of supporting development. Of course, in a society that overemphasizes the mind and has yet to fully address emotional intelligence, individuals must grow their own relationship with energy. And so here we are.

A while back someone told me, "You know, I've done years of therapy. Hell, I'm a relationship coach. Somewhere, I didn't want to associate with those crazy woo-woo people, so I stopped believing. But now, things have happened in my life, and talking isn't doing it. I'm realizing that underneath the words is a whole other place— energy—and I need to learn how to go there in order to feel better."

I've had many conversations that echo this sentiment. When it comes to personal development, talk therapy can be a great way to excavate pain while learning how to access belief systems and emotions. And yet after a while, because most experiences come with an energetic imprint, engaging energy integrates another level of healing. Many (many) times as people share the story of their lives, I see them spinning round and round to further entrench themselves. It's when they somehow move through the story and experience the energy inside—visualize, dance, cry, shout, draw, cough, laugh, breathe, shake, or just be—that shift happens. No matter how definite reality seems, delving underneath a story to interact with energy facilitates transformation at the core. Ultimately, the best way to learn how to navigate energy is by navigating energy.

When it comes to engaging energy, it's normal for resistance to be especially loud. But because the energetic world doesn't function in a linear way, learning to speak its language requires loosening up.

So please, give yourself permission to dance, laugh, shout, shake, sit, sing, dream, cough, scream, sob, make art, contemplate, speak in tongues, or do whatever so you can experience energy (as long as no hurting is involved). It's just us here. Who knows what healing we might grow?

EXERCISE: Find a song you love, turn up the volume, and dance or sing in your living room. Need inspiration? Check out "Let's Get Loud" by Jennifer Lopez. Can't do it? Examine any underlying fears that may be trying to keep you safe and small. See if they'll take a spin with you to develop some awareness regarding your relationship with energy.

Essential Navigation through Following Energy

Navigating energy is a creative practice that can become a form of art. Essential navigation includes noticing, connecting, receiving, holding, and following energy inside the body and in the context of daily life. More advanced navigation can include mediumship like channeling and transforming energy. At this moment, we're focusing on essential navigation through the five teachers of fear, awareness, choice, body, and intuition. Noticing fear and cultivating awareness help you remember choice and body wisdom so you can sense intuition and practice following energy. A whole enchilada, yes? I haven't forgotten about intention and surrender, but we're not there yet.

Navigating energy is quite a thing, which is why it needs a book. But the great news is you've already been learning how to navigate energy through the first five teachers. So take a deep breath and appreciate yourself. When a woman in labor says, "I can't do it," we respond, "You *are* doing it." Sensing your way through life one moment at a time *is* navigating the unknown. You are doing it.

There's one central tenet of following energy that everyone I know agrees with: following energy means staying behind the energy. Do not get ahead of the energy. This is much easier said than done in a fear-based society conditioned to manage anxiety through control.

We believe planning ahead and making things happen means success. But energy has its own sense of timing that can't be measured by a linear ruler or a ticking clock. To follow energy, we must live in the present moment and partner with unseen forces like intuition and body wisdom.

Learning how to get behind the energy of life challenges core foundations because it involves confronting our attachments. Whether the focus is a belief, a substance, a relationship, or even control itself, to be human is to be attached. And with attachment comes the fear of loss. Getting behind the energy and following it may involve letting go of something. When the stakes are high, letting go can be frightening.

If it's so challenging, why learn to follow energy? Anyone raising teenagers grapples with the desire to lock them away until their hormones regulate and their brains finish developing (to keep them safe, of course). Unfortunately, they aren't fully cooked until around age twenty-five. And so in the meantime, rather than cling to control as it erodes trust and generates lies (hello, Conflict Triangle), we can challenge ourselves by growing authentic relationship. Following energy brings us to the present moment when, step by step, we develop trust through building relationship. Thus, perhaps by age twenty-five, our future leaders have developed some authentic skills to move through life in a more balanced way.

PRACTICE: NOTICING ENERGY IN DAILY LIFE

Begin studying how you follow and get in front of energy every day. How do you prepare a meal, from sautéing onions to grilling fish and cooking rice? What gets in your way? A phone call? A screaming child? The thought that you're a lousy chef? How does it feel when you're midway through a project and someone voices (loud) opinions that block forward movement? What happens when you're driving and someone cuts you off?

Also spend some times noticing ways you get in front of energy. How do you cut people off, either in conversation or driving on the road? How patient are you with the progress of dinner when it's not your night to cook (and of course you're a better chef)? What fears, habits, and beliefs sabotage forward movement in your life? Getting a sense of how you naturally follow and get in front of energy will help develop your navigational skills.

So, How *Do* You Follow Energy?

During discussions, people often ask, "But how do I know when I'm following energy?" While ultimately, the answer depends on your own experience, I'll share some observations. Intuition is your best friend for learning how to navigate energy. If intuition involves learning to access your perception of a multisensory experience, energy is the multisensory experience itself. And so the way you follow energy will depend on how you perceive it. If you've been accessing intuition, you've already identified one or two of your strongest senses. The next step would be to begin a more focused noticing to follow the energy of something. Remember, you're noticing both inner and outer experiences.

For example, let's explore how you might follow the energy of your book intention. Perhaps you've identified a strong inner vision. You can go on an inner journey to follow your intention, noticing any images that stand out. Then as you move through daily life, you can sit with how that image might inform your intention. That's following energy. If you're a hearing person, you can pay attention to what words or messages arise as you contemplate your intention. Actually, journaling can help you receive an auditory message (it's like you're taking dictation!). You can also pay attention to outward conversations or songs on the radio to explore your intention.

If color is your thing, during inner work, ask to be shown what colors arise regarding your intention. Then remember to call upon those colors in daily life and also to notice when those colors appear in seemingly random ways. For those of you who strongly inhabit your body, ask to be shown where to hold the intention in your body. As you live life, remember to notice body sensations as a way to track what's happening with your intention.

Because energy is everywhere, we've all been interacting with energy. The shift is developing consciousness and committing to get behind energy. One key is growing a trust-based mutual relationship with whatever energy you follow. We're generating a conversation with energy, not offering a lecture, yes?

As you gather what you've been noticing about energy, imagine you're a detective keeping track of clues. Holding helps sort through everything to develop meaning and cultivate wisdom. At the same time, how you hold what you're noticing is also important. Energy needs room to move. Holding on to anything with a death grip kills circulation. So when following energy, remember to loosen up and allow for breathing room.

Because, by definition, following energy means staying behind it, recognizing when you've jumped ahead is essential. Often, getting ahead involves becoming overinvested or stuck in mental or emotional states. Fear regularly incites a leap into the future. So can bliss (deciding somebody is "the one" after three dates, ahem . . .). An arrogant or entitled attitude frequently gets ahead of itself. Overall, any kind of insistent knowing about a certain outcome, positive or negative, indicates getting ahead of the energy.

EXERCISE: Ask someone in your life to dance with you, ballroom style, holding hands and swinging each other around. Take turns leading and following. What comes more naturally for you?

Intuition helps locate where you are in relationship with energy. Getting ahead can feel like pushing against the wind. A voice inside might whisper to slow down. You could feel like you're forcing a square peg into a round hole. It's possible to assess relationship with energy through inner vision. Being out in front has a texture to it—perhaps rigid, righteous, or dogmatic. Once someone said, "I'm ahead of the energy if it tramples me. If I get out of the way, I don't feel crushed by it." Conversely, the absence of intuition can also help you locate yourself. If you're ahead of energy, there's nothing intuition can access. Stuck intuition is a great reminder to slow down, let go, back up, and begin again.

Part of navigating energy is learning how to recognize and facilitate flow. To follow energy means it must be moving. Thus, following energy means noticing movement. Stuck energy doesn't move. In fact, energy that isn't moving can become pretty dense. Conversely, flowing energy expresses strongly. After a practice to experience energy, we'll move inward to follow and shift energy through the body. And finally, we'll explore flow in daily life.

PRACTICE: A FELT SENSE OF FOLLOWING ENERGY

You can simulate following energy with this simple exercise. Choose any two objects. Push one object forward, imagining it as a relationship you're developing in your life. Contemplate decisions and actions that can fuel forward movement. Find a pace that feels good to you, noticing what happens when you push so slowly nothing happens and so quickly you lose contact. Experience what following energy feels like in your body.

Next, introduce the second object, imagining it is a difficult person in your life or a fear regarding your relationship. How does this second (interfering) object get in your way? What happens to your grip on the first object? Is forward movement possible? Play with the objects until you get a sense of blocked energy, especially noticing what getting ahead feels like inside your body.

Exploring Your Subtle Energy Body

Given its transformative power, the human body is an essential vehicle for learning how to follow energy. But first, some caveats. The relationship between subtle energy and body can, and does, fill many volumes of books representing a lifetime (or more) of study. As an energy worker, I have deep respect for the subtle energy body. These few paragraphs don't amount to a drop in the ocean of knowledge on this matter. Yet everyone needs to begin somewhere. Our first step focuses on navigating subtle energy through your own body.

In discussing body and energy, I think it's important to mention chakras. Many esoteric traditions recognize subtle energy centers in the body, most commonly called chakras, from the Sanskrit word for "wheel" or "disk." The origins of chakras come from Hindu and yoga (Tantra) traditions, and Western New Age philosophy offers new variations. In general, most philosophies agree that there are seven major energy centers located in specific regions of the body: base of spine, pelvis, solar plexus, heart, throat, center of forehead/third eye, and top of head/crown. Some believe each chakra holds both individual and archetypal information. Some also relate chakras to specific colors, sounds, mantras, bodily functions, and more. Most traditions encourage interacting with chakras to develop consciousness.

While I believe in chakras, it won't surprise you that I'm more interested in individual experiences of subtle energy. As a healing practitioner who supports authentic meaning, my role is to help you experience the color of your own heart chakra, or the place inside that fuels your power. Although some schools of thought believe that energy always wants to move up through the body, I'm not sold on this idea. Or that developing consciousness means transcending the body at all. For me, the meaning of the chakras comes through direct relationship. To expect a chakra to look or act a certain way is getting ahead of your unique healing process.

Energy is alive and dynamic. As energy changes, so can your experience of it. One moment, your heart chakra may be purple and in the next, it's pink. Shifts in awareness change energy fields. I've personally traveled from the depths of hell into radiant bliss in the time it takes to flip a coin. Energy is wild. It doesn't want to be caged by expectations based on a *should*. Energy won't move if it's constricted; it needs freedom to lead the way.

PRACTICE: CONNECTING WITH YOUR ENERGY CENTERS

Go to your spiritual area and create sacred space. Move inward into your body. Ask to be shown your own energy centers. You can move through your chakras from the base through the top of your head or connect directly with a chakra that draws your attention. You may also explore a chakra that needs healing regarding your intention. Notice any images, colors, words, or sensations. When you've completed, express gratitude and close your circle.

Subtle Energy Plus Body Equals
Jennifer Sugarwoman

As a serious student of subtle energy, I've been blessed with great teachers. I first met Jennifer Sugarwoman several years into my apprenticeship when she became a co-owner of Oneisha Healing Tools. Jennifer is a spiritual counselor and bodyworker with more than fifteen years of experience in a variety of healing arts modalities, including meditation, embodied movement, and Maitri Breathwork. She served as my mentor for more than ten years, and her mastery in navigating subtle body energy continually inspires me.

Jennifer recently described how she helped a client who had spent many years working with someone else. That practitioner often encouraged the client to just "be with" a particular core wound that repeatedly arose. Rather than continue the cycle, Jennifer asked the client, "You've been with this pattern for about fifteen years. What else would you like to do with it?"

In the beginning, it's crucial for people to identify core patterns and recognize violating experiences. Here, working with fear, awareness, and the body can be of great assistance. But Jennifer believes that someone who "knows the pattern from the inside out doesn't need to collapse with it all the time." The next step is to ask different questions: How do they move and shift the energy? How can it become a wise guiding light instead of a place of collapse? This articulates an important developmental arc within a personal healing journey.

Once you get to really know the flavor and texture of a wound, you can choose to take responsibility for tending to it. Taking responsibility might mean establishing healthy boundaries, nourishing yourself, or shifting energy from inside. Jennifer said, "So many times we come from ego and ask, 'Why is this happening to me? Why am I feeling this way?' And those are great questions, but they're overused compared to 'What is this energy about?' and 'Do I need to move it or do I need to let it envelop me?'" Learning how to work with energy involves connecting with your body.

EXERCISE: Contemplate your core wounds or patterns. Consider the role you often assume in the Conflict Triangle. What might taking responsibility look like? Remember to identify your needs and generate support.

Twist and Shout: Moving Subtle Energy through Your Body

Moving energy begins with locating it in the body. Often during an individual session when someone describes a core pattern or wound, I ask, "And where does this live inside your body?" A hand almost always gravitates to a particular spot. I ask the same question regarding a story or mental process: "And where does this experience live in your body?" Again, a hand moves instinctually. Transitioning to table work provides an opportunity to feel the energy directly.

Jennifer elaborated, "If people can access the energy in some way either verbally or through hands-on healing or shake it or move it or sing it or sound it or do something that begins to unwind the current, then the dynamic potency of the energy starts to have a trail of movement." Conscious expression helps energy move.

Allowing ourselves to get loud is a leap. From childhood, we're taught to shut down. Children should be seen and not heard. Crying makes people uncomfortable. Wild bigness threatens the status quo. The first time I participated in Maitri Breathwork, I screamed like a banshee for at least thirty minutes. While it felt *great* in the moment, as I emerged with sweat pouring down my cheeks, my hair frizzy and knotted, I became self-conscious. Just then, a smiling assistant greeted me with a thumbs-up and said, "Good work!" This encouraged me to trust my experience.

To help you get more comfortable embracing your wild side, find some kindred people and practice getting loud. This isn't about primal screaming in a grocery store but instead about locating safe and conscious places to hold your unfolding authenticity. There are many forms of energy work. Dance. Yoga. Painting. Breathwork. Martial arts. Acupuncture. Individual sessions. Here, I would encourage you to listen to your heart but be skeptical of anyone promising the moon in just three visits.

EXERCISE: In my energy-friendly community at the Center for Sacred Studies, shaking, laughing, coughing, sounding, drawing, envisioning, singing, sobbing, dancing, drumming, belching (!), and speaking nonsensically within sacred settings are normal ways we regularly move energy. Identify three ways you instinctively shift energy. How might your intuition help you discover more ways?

Noticing Integrates Subtle Body Awareness

After an energy-moving experience, it's important to notice any changes, sensations, colors, or textures in the body. It's normal to feel lighter inside, or perhaps experience tingling sensations. Sometimes people feel nauseous or achy. I've been taught that one hour of energy work is comparable to eight hours of digging a ditch. Drinking water or bathing with sea salt is helpful. After big experiences or when feeling sensitive, it's wise to avoid public places for at least a day—no rock concerts!

Taking a moment to notice the difference within is key. Jennifer explained, "That's where the embodiment process can grow. If we're just going to the next thing and next thing and next thing, then we're still oblivious to what's really happening in the patterning." Consciousness needs awareness to grow.

Noticing energy movement also gives your mind a job to do and might help barking dogs quiet down as your ego adjusts to consciousness awakening. Additionally, contemplating different methods of shifting energy illuminates options for the future. In fact, the ways you shift energy become your very own healing tools. Born out of relationship with your individual energy body, these are your unique tools of navigation.

The Heart of Navigating Subtle Body Energy

Imagine you've grown some sea legs in moving subtle energy. Your body likes to shift energy through shaking and coughing. Yoga and drawing also help you express. Through these processes, your body somehow feels lighter inside. Your body is becoming a conscious tuning fork for noticing energy. Your sensitivity has increased. You trust your intuition more.

You start to notice that certain emotions or experiences weigh you down. In the past, you might have dismissed it, but now the discomfort gets your attention. You feel stuffed, as if you've overeaten. Unusually strange or grumpy thoughts haunt you. You get a pounding headache. One minute you're fine, the next you're drowning in feelings that won't leave—this is not normal for you. You have nightmares. Your mind won't stop spinning about an interaction or relationship. You can't sleep. Your stomach clenches in certain situations. You're learning that these are signals that it's time to go inside and shift your energy.

At this point it's possible to expand your awareness to multiple levels of consciousness. As you move inward, you can also hold an awareness of moving inward. As you start to experience energy in your heart—perhaps it begins as grief and you start to cry—you can also hold an awareness that grief is running through you. You experience the sensation of grief without becoming lost in it. You can invoke different healing tools to engage this grief. You ask questions. You cough something up. Your body shakes. The grief shifts from chilling cold into a warm tingling sensation.. You notice the warmth and breathe deeply to expand it. As you're breathing, you recognize a sense of gratitude. You feel gratitude moving through your heart to envelop your whole body. You bask in gratitude for a while. Even in this state, you remain aware of where you are.

Welcome to the inner world of navigating energy.

In this place of meta-consciousness, the mind becomes a healing tool of its own. Questions become a vehicle to track energy: What am I feeling? What am I noticing about how I'm feeling? Do any body parts feel constricted? Is this energy a part of me, or does it feel distinct? Can I move that energy with a sound or a positive thought? How does this energy want to move through my body—through my feet or my hands or out of the top of my head? Some energy shifts in an instant. Other energy may benefit from professional support.

EXERCISE: Breathe in the possibility of navigating your own subtle energy. For fun, find Joan Osborne's "Love is Alive" and dance around the room.

PRACTICE: NAVIGATING YOUR OWN SUBTLE ENERGY

Go to your spiritual area, preferably with some soft, instrumental music, and create sacred space. Call upon the energy of something you'd like to explore, but nothing too painful. Move inward to where this energy lives in your body. Interact with this energy, remembering to call upon all your senses. If it wants to move, play with finding pathways of release through your body. If it wishes to remain, bathe it in a beautiful color. Remember choice and gentleness, no need to rush.

When you're ready, notice your experience. How does your body feel now? How did you navigate this energy? Draw or journal your experience. Look out for barking dogs. Offer gratitude and close your circle.

Shift Happens: Moving Energy in Daily Life

While it may take time to notice subtle energy within our bodies, often our outer relationships clearly reflect both energetic fluidity and places we're blocked. We project unresolved trauma, core wounds, and unconscious patterning outward into the fabric of relationships. With partners, parents, coworkers, children, and friends. Through generating a work life or earning money. Core patterns especially live in the *how* of everyday life—how we relate to people, decisions, jobs, and creativity.

And so, just as it's possible to identify, express, and heal core wounds inside your body, you can recognize and tend to the negative patterns those wounds create in your daily life. "It's not about making something wrong, it's about how we shift it," said Jennifer. "First, it's how to recognize that what is outside is mirrored inside. If I can find that place, then I'm not going to be stuck in the outward projection of it and I'm going to take the responsibility to move it." Here, studying a particular energy helps activate choice. Rather than reacting unconsciously, potentially collapsing into a core pattern or wound, you can decide how to respond.

So what might shifting the energy look like in daily life? First, a regular practice of moving inward provides a safe place to shift energy. There are also a myriad of ways to transform energy without going too wild. Take a brisk walk. Journal. Practice yoga. Soak in a hot bath. Call a friend. Make art. Love your pet. My Rhythm & Motion Dance Workout teacher, Amara Tabor-Smith, encourages booty-movement therapy. "The next time you're in an argument, stop, shake your booty, and see what happens!" If I'm feeling off at Trader Joe's, you might find me singing Journey's "Don't Stop Believin'" under my breath. Creative expression is essential for energy movement. Make shift happen, baby!

EXERCISE: Journal or draw a core wound. Explore how that wound permeates your relationships. What would taking responsibility for shifting it look like? Remember to identify needs and seek support.

The Gift of Holding, Letting Go, and Following Synchronicity in Daily Life

So much in life depends on our capacity to hold. How much and how long we can hold people, projects, and decisions. The way we hold relationship. And especially how we hold ourselves. Our ability to let go and accept loss also matters. To find inroads when we face dead ends. To relax as change breaks us open. The paradox of energy work is that we need to become whole enough to get out of our own way. So we can follow. Being whole enough to let go is how we cultivate a different approach to life.

Developing consciousness reflects the dance between holding and letting go. Moving inward to transform energy offers foundational practice. And yet, when it comes to daily life, our attachment to what we're holding—relationships, children, health, money, and survival itself—makes letting go especially difficult. Then transforming energy in daily life isn't only singing a song at Trader Joe's but might also include raising children, getting divorced, navigating cancer, or leaving home for a job. And here's where consciously following energy becomes tangible. Our capacity to hold fears and wounds clears the way to follow energy in daily life. Although clearer vision doesn't guarantee smooth sailing through life's changing waters, it does strengthen navigation.

Turning Dead Ends into Doorways

When it comes to following energy in your daily life, synchronistic events mediate holding and letting go. You can hold space to follow something, calling upon awareness, intuition, and body wisdom to deepen your study. When the energy is flowing, events begin happening. Conversely, life stagnating can reflect a need to let go. As you shift between holding and letting go, you generate choices that fuel expansion. Energy merges with daily life to create a trail of potential meaning. Opportunity arrives. Here, because you're human and often attached to whatever you're holding, it's crucial not to jump to any conclusions. Hold loosely by staying conscious of the whole enchilada. Don't get ahead of the energy. If you do, pull yourself back and begin again, always remembering the power of letting go. At some point, the energy seems to ripen. If at that moment you hold steady and keep following, you receive a healing gift tailored just for you.

Of course, this gift can't be your sole motivation for becoming conscious or it won't arrive. In fact, there's no way to predict what the gift is or whether it will come in a tangible form. Following energy may or may not provide the outcome you want, though it does generate healing tools along the way. But the truth is that when you truly let go and follow energy, magic enters your life.

Synchronicity shocks you with lightning-bolt surprises that break you open and then fill you with awe. The grief of letting go births exactly what you need to sustain the dream that emerges in daily life. Seemingly dead ends become doorways. You arrive at places inside and out that somehow fulfill a promise you didn't know your soul had made. And often these realizations crystallize during an unexpected aha moment of completion.

It's after following something step by step with love and commitment that pieces of what you've been holding converge to bless you. In that instance, you notice how you've grown. You recognize how following has led you through challenges for your highest good and deepest healing. These awakenings inspire gratitude over hubris because you haven't held on to an end result with a death grip. You haven't manipulated anything into existence. You've been staying in the unknown and following without expectation. And from that state of being, the realization that arrives is a gift unto itself.

Living in the unknown requires holding more—especially more discomfort. If the work of consciousness means allowing your heart to break open, these aha moments of completion arrive as a healing balm. These moments restore faith. They initiate gratitude and deepen trust. These moments represent magic. They are grace. They contain messages. These moments mirror the next level of development in your life.

I encourage you to bask in these moments of completion. Celebrate! Appreciate the gifts and notice the wisdom. Avoid measuring these moments based on any outside scale but instead recognize meaning for yourself. Then gently let them go. Because what often arrives after rebirthing yourself is that you begin again, entering larger and usually scarier unknowns. Here, newfound trust generates courage in your capacity to relax into the stretch and hold more.

....

EXERCISE: Contemplate an aha moment that's come from following something—not pushed or manipulated but allowed. What gifts and lessons arrived with this moment? How did your life change because of what you learned?

....

Rebirth

I've mentioned my relationship with conscious pregnancy and birth. Whether it was being a doula; coordinating an on-call, hospital-based midwifery service; or co-facilitating holistic childbirth preparation groups, helping prospective parents develop awareness and inner authority was a way to strengthen the world. As the nexus in a family, empowered parents can embody the tipping point for awakening consciousness. But after many years, I'd merged with birth so completely there was little room for other healing work. So when the on-call midwifery service I coordinated was closed, I decided to relinquish every role I held in the birth world to say goodbye.

I spent six months dancing and writing through the grief of letting go. With some distance, other seeds of healing work began to sprout. Writing about Practical Spirituality emerged. Sacred Dance blossomed. I started facilitating women's circles and providing small-business support to holistic practitioners. I began assistant teaching at a facilitator training for Maitri Breathwork, a transformative process developed by Jyoti and Russell Park now housed at the Center for Sacred Studies. Dancing-Tree Consulting arrived with many branches to hold people.

One year later, I experienced a surprise moment of awakening while assisting a weekend Maitri Breathwork facilitator training. As I listened to instruction about Stanislav Grof's foundational work within transpersonal psychology, a spark of inquiry arrived: if breathers can access prenatal material during breathwork, how might the role of mother or life-giver also be experienced? The question blew me open with a blast of electric heat. In an instant, distinct parts of myself—energy worker, student of women's spirituality, mother, doula, breathwork facilitator—reorganized into cohesiveness. It was as if these relationships had grown close enough within me to meet and ignite inside a question: Hey, where's the mother in breathwork?

Though I felt like a wildly alive wire, because I was there to assist (and not fall over), I breathed slowly until the flames of realization settled. Again suddenly, shining through the cracks of my shifting reality, my heart recognized a familiar energy: birth. Beloved birth. Birth was with me again. In the distance, my poor ego started thrashing. Hadn't I spent the last year saying goodbye to birth? I thought I'd let birth go. Buried. Gone. How could birth just, *poof,* return? A cool, gentle wave of compassion soothed misgivings as my smiling heart welcomed birth home. From that place, I recognized the thread of birth running through me. How birth transforms consciousness. How, underneath everything, birth remained true in my life.

At lunch, I sank into a nearby couch to find some equilibrium. I turned my head and discovered Jyoti sitting on my left. Jyoti is the spiritual director of Center for Sacred Studies and the cofounder of Stargate School and Maitri Breathwork. To find Jyoti in the country, much less sitting on her own, unoccupied, was unusual. And so I asked her about the potential role of a life-giver during breathwork. Jyoti immediately cocked her head to the side and sent me a piercing glance. "What an excellent question to live into. I'm not sure if anyone has studied it." Years later, as I hold Maitri Breathwork for the general public and remain on the teaching staff for the facilitator training, I'm still enjoying living into the question.

To this day, I'm not sure if birth died that year for me or not. Maybe my grip simply loosened enough for birth to fly free and return transformed. I am continually surprised by how birth presents itself in my life. I never thought I'd be a doula again, certainly not at my beloved Nicole's birth and certainly not twice (in six weeks) while writing a book. In fact, the other day birth came calling again—my pregnant sister-in-law just asked me to be her doula next month. Surprise! While I might need to take a deep breath and ground, I no longer cage birth with the expectation of how it must appear in my life or worry about when it will arrive. Perhaps this ultimate letting go has allowed me to follow birth and to trust the ways it remembers me. With deep gratitude, I simply say yes. I'm here. I'm here.

How Getting Ahead Can Hurt

Toward the end of my conversation with Jennifer, we discussed the importance of holding so the potency of the energy has time to build. Jennifer said, "I might feel a client has a huge energy of abuse, but I'm not going to say anything right away. It's important to stay with the energy that's present or you can scare the heck out of someone. That's getting ahead of the energy."

The very (very!) next day, I received a phone call from June, who attends an ongoing women's Sacred Dance group. Happily married with two young children, she had treated herself to a session with a psychic for her birthday the day before. June's intention was to connect with her beloved deceased parents. Instead, the psychic launched into dire predictions, essentially saying June's marriage was doomed.

June's normally vibrant voice cracked with tears. "He said not to worry. That after going through a horrible time and basically divorcing, I would find the true love of my life. Staci, I love my husband. I'm not saying we don't have some issues, but overall, we're very happy. I don't know what to make of any of this."

I empathized with June, and then we reviewed a recent incident when a doctor raised the subject of cancer screening in a frightening way, catapulting June into exploring how fear informs her life. I said, "So I'm wondering, what's fear trying to teach you now?"

"That this psychic is giving me some *Eat Pray Love* story of loss and redemption. My husband *is* the love of my life. With two kids under five, we're tired, but who isn't?"

"And June, let's say for a moment this psychic is correct and next year your marriage has a bump, especially because it's normal with two young kids. How has this psychic reading supported your healing?"

"It hasn't. It's just planted these seeds of doubt and fear. And it's created extra work because now I need to process this experience. I'm pissed off. I'm certainly going to give this guy some feedback. Just like I did with the doctor."

June and I explored her ability to speak up for herself in difficult situations as a helpful gift. We also compared her two experiences, noticing June's speed in shifting to an empowered perspective regarding the psychic. I said, "And here you were trying to give yourself a birthday present. Some present!" With that, we laughed and moved on.

EXERCISE: Remember when someone used fear about a potential future to turn you into a victim, perhaps to establish power or to gain your compliance. What happened? What energy from this experience remains with you? How can you shift it?

Navigating Energy as Artful Living

Learning how to follow and navigate energy isn't easy, but it's worth the effort. A journey of awakening can be intense *and* exciting. Noticing fear and cultivating awareness help you remember choice and body wisdom so you can sense intuition and practice navigating energy throughout life. Getting behind the energy of your own healing facilitates wholeness. Following energy beyond a certain outcome allows everyone access to healing in a meaningful way.

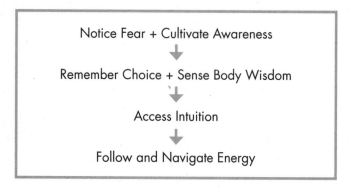

Notice Fear + Cultivate Awareness

Remember Choice + Sense Body Wisdom

Access Intuition

Follow and Navigate Energy

So much about consciously holding and letting go depends on our grip. Last night, my family visited friends with a newborn. When our friends recognized their baby's cry as expressing painful gas, they began trying different body positions to soothe their child. Within five minutes, the baby was calm and alert. Navigating the energy of a newborn requires complete devoted attention. This baby's life rests in her parents' hands. But no matter the firmness necessary with this kind of attention, it's still possible to hold in a relaxed way.

Shifting relationship with your core fears, wounds, and patterns by navigating their energy from the inside out facilitates individual authority. We grow responsibility—the ability to respond—to how life unfolds. Practicing spirituality becomes artful living. Once you become aware of your wounds and can shift your relationship, a question emerges: What energy in your life are you going to follow? This choice point becomes a diving-off place to explore the teacher of intention.

ENERGY GUIDELINES, YOUR INTEGRATIVE QUESTIONS

- How do you experience energy inside yourself and throughout daily life?

- How do you follow and get ahead of energy in your life?

- What are some ways you notice, shift, and move energy through your body?

- What's your relationship with holding and letting go?

- How does synchronicity help you follow energy in daily life?

- How are you following, holding, and navigating the energy of your book intention?

9

Intention: The Root and Tip of Embodying Consciousness

As you've moved through fear, awareness, choice, body, intuition, and energy, I hope you've been following the intention you created at the beginning of this book. If intention has not been your focal point, it's okay. Forgive yourself. Intention can be elusive and almost easy to dismiss. Wherever you are, this chapter will further your relationship with intention as a guide in your life.

In my healing practice, I've noticed that at some point most people lose sight of their specific intention. We write down intentions. We narrow them to one word. Groups begin with everyone stating intentions. And still, over and over again people not only forget the key to their awakening, but they also forget to turn the key and ignite consciousness through taking action. They forget to hold, fuel, and follow their intentions.

I'm not judging anyone for this lapse. It's just that when it comes to intention, my eyebrow is permanently raised at attention. What is it about an intention that makes us forget and effectively fall back asleep into unconsciousness? Has our frenetic, multitasking culture damaged our ability to hold a focus? Has the instant gratification of technology like texting and Facebook stunted the patience we need to grow something over time, including ourselves?

I've heard that becoming conscious is a process of remembering and forgetting and remembering again. The beauty of intention is that it helps you remember who you are. The challenge of holding and following an intention is that it leads you through the depths of the unknown, and it's in those depths where you can get tired or lost so that you forget and fall back asleep. Yet especially when you're in an unconscious place, remembering your intention helps you wake up and find yourself again. Intention can mediate the natural remembering and forgetting of awakening consciousness.

Have you ever had a conversation where someone's wisdom washes over you like deep, fresh water, magnificent but impossible to hold? It's as if that person is speaking directly to your soul, but to catch the wisdom, you need to back up and begin the conversation again. For me, an intention magnifies your emerging wisdom. Intentions like trust, strength, commitment, and motherhood create a direct line of communication between you and your soul.

In the previous chapter, you discovered a whole-enchilada teacher: noticing fear and cultivating awareness helps you remember choice and body wisdom so you can sense intuition and practice following energy. You touched the heart of consciously following the energy of something. From here, questions arrive: What energy will you choose to follow? Are you going to follow your wounds? It seems to me that following wounds spins people around until they become lost. What helps you move beyond your wounds? Where else might you focus your attention?

These questions lead into the realm of intention. Noticing fear cultivates awareness to remember choice and body wisdom while accessing intuition so you can follow the energy of an intention. Practicing spirituality happens through navigating an intention. Intention guides you through the depths of yourself and daily life experience so you can embody your own soul's wisdom.

PRACTICE: GROUND YOURSELF

Take a moment to breathe into your body and ground yourself. Remember the intention you created at the beginning of this book. It's okay to hone it again to reflect what you need to learn at this moment, but make sure that the two intentions connect.

Following Intention through Book Writing

My intention has been to wholeheartedly serve all my relationships through writing this book. This includes you the reader, people in my life, and the eight guides. I've been fortunate to learn from some incredible people—wise spiritual teachers and healing practitioners. I've held an intention to shine a light on these people so you could experience them too.

But then as I began to write about fear, baby Dyllan's heart condition was discovered. As our community galvanized to support Dyllan and her family, I let go of interviewing mentors. During Stargate training when a facilitator took emergency leave, we were reminded that sometimes a teacher gets pulled away and a student must find the strength to step forward and take care of things. In alignment with Dyllan's healing, I trusted it was up to me to grow another level of relationship with what remained—the eight teachers from the book. Batter up.

After more than two hundred days in an intensive care unit, Dyllan has moved to a regular hospital room and will soon go home. With schedules loosening, I was able to visit with Jyoti, and four days later, I met with Darlene Hunter. Since both women are busy world travelers often serving schools, communities, and organizations from different points across the globe, it feels like Jyoti and Darlene have come together to help us explore the root and tip of following intention.

Intention as a Choice to Hold Pivotal Moments with Fierce Love

I was sitting across from Diana, a beloved client who had spent nearly a decade reclaiming herself from abusive relationships through a variety of healing modalities. Her latest intention was embodiment. Diana had recently met a caring man, and she was on the cusp of actualizing a dream regarding her work life. And what had all her attention in this moment? She was feeling immobilized by mean, scary thoughts telling her she was worthless and destined to fail. I listened awhile and then said, "Diana, you know these voices well. When are you going to tell them to sit down and shut up?"

That same day, I received an email from another fabulous woman, Jade. She had been holding an intention to thrive. Jade's a gifted photographer with a flair for organization. When she's focused, she's able to make a good living in her field with flexible hours that support her creative life. And despite her many years of healing physical trauma through nutrition, dance, and somatic therapy, Jade's email was full of fear and hesitation. She was stuck.

What the hell was going on?! With all the personal healing tools these two tremendously gifted women had developed, why couldn't they move forward? Rather than recognizing how she was embodying herself, Diana was allowing fearful voices to beat her down. Jade stopped thriving when she became immobilized by fear.

There comes a point in developing consciousness where you need to get tough with yourself. Not tough as in mean or judgmental but tough as in fiercely loving. Where part of growing wisdom is to feel the fear and move forward anyway. To notice the negative voices, love them, cradle some of them while they cry and tell the others to sit down. Part of healing involves re-parenting your inner wounded child. To hold challenge, pay attention, call upon gentleness, and move forward some more. You've spent enough time getting to know your wounds to arrive at a question: Are you going to collapse inside your wounds or put your attention elsewhere? As writer Maya Angelou has said, "When we know better, we do better." There comes a time when consciousness means claiming responsibility for your life.

EXERCISE: What are three ways you collapse into your wounds? List three ways you can activate your book intention instead. How will you love yourself more fiercely?

Intention can guide you through pivotal life moments to help you stay awake and take responsibility. To illustrate this point, Jyoti recalled her powerful experience at a *Peter Pan* movie showing with an audience of children. "There's that moment when Tinker Bell is on the edge of death and Peter Pan turns and speaks directly to the audience saying, 'Do you believe? Do you believe in fairies? If you believe, clap your hands. Don't let Tink die!'"

Jyoti remembered, "These children—the innocence of our life—started to say, 'I believe in fairies. I believe in fairies. I believe in fairies!' . . . louder and louder until we were hollering it. The energy and the feeling, you could feel it enter the whole theater, is that all of oneself is behind that intention, I believe, I believe, I believe in fairies.

"And then all of Tinker Bell's magic returns. All of her life, her passion returns. She begins to tinker and twinkle, and she flies all around the audience. All the children are laughing and clapping and life is good. . . . That energy filled our bodies. It filled our minds. It took away doubt. That, for me, is a kernel of what intention can do."

Jyoti's story reveals the power of intention as a kind of fierce love: I believe, I believe, I believe in fairies. Such wholehearted commitment acts as a steadying force, even in the face of death. It also shifts the energy regarding Tinker Bell, both inside her and around her. Jyoti said, "True intention and prayer doesn't go anywhere unless it's generated by feeling." While believing in fairies doesn't guarantee that Tinker Bell will live, love can help everyone learn to fly in their own way.

Intention can help you hold challenging points in your life with fierce love. Whether you're experiencing loss or rebirth, intention represents your choice to remain awake through transformation. Intention is a specific commitment you make to yourself such as thriving, embodying healing, or growing trust. When something happens, intention can help you sort through life to decipher meaning. Intention also helps you practice fiercely loving yourself to grow self-worth. So you can learn how to trust yourself enough to take flight.

What if you held intention as a spark of energy? Something alive you can invite into your life as a guiding force like Tinker Bell's light? How might you hold an intention if you believed it could facilitate life? Where would you focus your fierce love? Intention pinpoints your choice. Intention casts your vote.

EXERCISE: Consider your feelings, thoughts, and actions on a typical day. Where are you *really* focusing your attention? How can your book intention help you grow fierce love? Remember the whole enchilada.

Intention as the Root and the Tip

As we delve deeper, it's important to clarify some different levels of intention. Darlene Hunter recently reminded me, "I can have an intention to get in my car and go the store, but what we really need to discover is: What is my walking prayer? What is my life service for? That's my overall intention." For Darlene, cofounder of Kayumari community and international teacher, certified Maitri Breathwork facilitator, and chief executive officer at the Center for Sacred Studies, begins each day with an overall prayer and intention: "I am in service to people, to the planet, to the Divine Mother. Because whatever you put at the tip of the arrow is where the whole arrow is going to line up."

Jyoti added to this understanding, "Intention also gives the arrow direction. If you don't have direction, the arrow zips all over the place, and it might do something but it would not do it with power intended." An intention is what helps you follow energy. Darlene said, "If you're behind your intention or prayer or whatever the focus is, then you can stay on track. Without a focus, without an intention, without a prayer, energy is random." Without a conscious intention, an unconscious belief or feeling may try to dictate reality.

Jyoti added another dimension to intention: "Intention is the root. It's the root of the tree." This goes back to the beginning of the book where I outlined an *And* way of life that includes simultaneously living in the present moment *and* holding focus for an outcome *and* staying in the unknown regarding outcome. Intention grounds us, inviting us to be aware of the present and the future without getting ahead of anything. Intention activates an *And* way of life. Thus intention is both the tip of the arrow and the root of the tree.

EXERCISE: What sits at the tip of your arrow? What keeps you grounded in life?

Rooted Intention

Though she is not an indigenous woman, Jyoti's understanding of intention is based on more than twenty years of relationship with indigenous ways of healing. "For First Nations people, intention is everything," explained Jyoti. "Everything we do with our prayer has to do with intention." Jyoti spoke about becoming a sacred tobacco pipe carrier through Eugene Blackbear Sr., an elder Cheyenne medicineman and her spiritual grandfather. A pipe carrier is someone who offers healing prayers with tobacco to help people.

In preparation for receiving the pipe, Jyoti was asked to sit on a mountaintop for four days every year for four years, fasting with no food or water so she could cultivate receptivity and responsibility. When Grandpa Eugene presented the pipe, it came with new restrictions: "There were certain things I could and couldn't do if I wanted to keep a clear intention behind the use of my pipe." Following these restrictions demonstrated Jyoti's commitment to staying behind the healing energy of her pipe.

Jyoti's pipe story reveals how the root of an intention can connect an individual with generations of people through prayer. It's unusual for a nonindigenous person to be given a pipe, and it signifies a commitment to serving humanity through a specific lineage of healing. "If I'm going to pick up my pipe to pray for somebody, I'm going to do that the way it was handed down to me," said Jyoti. "When I do that, my intention connects with the intention of those who have prayed that way for generations and generations. Back to where the pipe told that first one how to take care of it. To connect with the power that gave the pipe to us to pray. If I decide to take shortcuts—'Well I don't understand that one' or 'I don't agree with that one'—or start to do a level of personal interpretation, then I start to move my line of intention away from the center of itself, and my prayer will reflect that. It wouldn't have the same level of power."

Jyoti likens this process to dialing a phone number. If I decide your number is 111-1112 and it's really 111-1111, then I can dial that first number, but I won't reach you. I won't be fulfilling my intention to connect with you if I don't call your actual phone number.

Jyoti illustrates intention as a root. Intention helps connect Jyoti back to an original source of power so she can be of service to the generations before and after her. Jyoti's intention holds and sustains her in the present moment as she offers healing prayers while sitting in the unknown mystery. Because these prayers are to help people, a clear, strong intention becomes crucial. Jyoti said, "Intention is one of the switches that you flip that's going to set a way of life into a being state." Darlene's root intention and daily prayer also reflect unwavering commitment. As nonindigenous women in service through many First Nations healing ways, the integrity of their prayers rests on a clear relationship with intention.

While you may not be committing to a life of service, Jyoti and Darlene can inspire you to discover your root. Darlene said, "I remember asking myself what I was supposed to do and wondering about my path. And then I was told, 'Look down, you're standing on it.'" At this moment, your path of healing has led you to this book as a way to explore conscious relationship. I invite you to sit with how your book intention might relate to an intention for your life. If you feel an immediate connection between your book and potential life intention, wonderful! It's also okay if you don't. Jyoti traveled to sit on a mountaintop for four days for four consecutive years to grow a relationship with an intention. There's no need to rush, just begin to live into the question.

PRACTICE: THE ROOT OF YOUR INTENTION

Go to your spiritual area and create sacred space. Remember your book intention as a choice to love yourself fiercely. Allow your intention to fill your body. Next, spend time drawing, journaling, or contemplating your intention to discover the essence of what it holds. If you're following a one-word theme, the connection may be clear. If you're holding an intention regarding daily life, consider meaning. For example, what would it mean if you could meet a partner, grow a career, or become a parent? Inside the gift you seek may be the essence you need to develop.

Once you identify an essence, close your eyes and enter a natural setting. Ask to be shown how this essence might relate to a root intention for your whole life. As always, notice any colors, words, images, sensations, or textures. When you're ready, open your eyes and draw or journal your experience and then close your circle.

Remember one thing from your experience and hold it as you move through everyday life. Begin to study how the root of your intention permeates your life. Notice your fears to generate awareness. Pay attention to choice and body wisdom, moving inward to shift and release energy. Notice how synchronicity appears to expand your conversation. As you connect with your root, don't forget to apply any lessons you learn to your book intention.

Open Focus: An Orgasmic Intention

We've been delving into intention as the root and the tip of a choice to love fiercely. While discovering the meaning of intention is key, the spiritual needs the practical to fully enter daily life. How you hold an intention bridges relationship and also turns practicing spirituality into an enjoyable, and potentially ecstatic, form of art.

Because the practical world invites us to get earthy, I'm going to trust that we've traveled far enough together to get a little more intimate. For many years as I've sat with how to hold an intention, I intuitively hear two words: open focus. And what arrives with it is to approach holding intention like an orgasm. Yes, an orgasm. First, please note that I'm communicating here as a woman. And I recognize that not all women can have orgasms. But regardless, stay with me and imagine.

Over the years, I've taken an informal poll and pretty much every woman I've asked agrees that orgasms don't often just happen. Usually, at some point during a moment of intimacy a woman decides if she'd like to have an orgasm or not. In a subtle way, an orgasm involves a choice.

What does it take to experience an orgasm? Here, I don't mean an attuned lover (or a great vibrator!). I'm asking, what needs to happen in a woman's mind, body, and spirit so she can open to an orgasm? Often, relaxing is key. If a woman goes after an orgasm with a scrunched up, willful—give it to me *now*, damn it—kind of attitude, chances are, it won't happen. An orgasm requires receptivity. It asks a woman to be in the moment. So she can experience her body. And notice what feels good. By trusting her instincts. An orgasm likes authenticity. A woman who can identify her needs while remembering a sense of humor. To stay in the moment and follow the energy as it awakens. So she can let go. An orgasm is an opportunity to practice opening while holding a focus on an intention.

And so if it resonates, I invite you to approach intention like having an orgasm. In fact, what if we held navigating energy in daily life as an orgasmic journey? I bet our eight teachers would happily support moving in that direction! Along these lines, holding an intention can begin with remembering two words: open focus (or one: orgasm!). Be receptive in the present moment but stay vigilant about the direction you're headed.

EXERCISE: What would happen if you approached holding your intention like having an orgasm? How clear is your focus? How do you relax, open, and let go?

Action Fuels Your Intention and Inspires Synchronicity

An intention needs more than your belief to come to life; it requires you to demonstrate commitment by taking tangible steps to actualize your dream. Jyoti has heard the Dalai Lama say, "Prayer is good, but prayer must have action."

"That's what intention is," said Jyoti. "It's the engine that gives focus and direction to a heart's wish."

Darlene extrapolated, "There's an expression that says, 'Trust in God but tie up your camel.' I can have an intention that is prayer, but what's the action that's going to get behind an intention happening? Because if you have that intention, you need the arrow and the shaft and the feathers on the end, and you need a bow."

Cultivating an *And* way of life means holding fear alongside a heartfelt commitment to an intention. Then the practice becomes showing up fully in the moment without expectation to follow what happens. To track where the energy of an intention is leading in order to decide how to respond next. Here, teachers like awareness, choice, body, and intuition are essential guides for perceiving and relating with an intention. And there may be other teachers involved: commitment, anger, forgiveness, passion, humility, gratitude.

Throughout this journey, synchronicity is a central messenger that reflects, mediates, and directs flow between holding a vision and actualizing a reality. Experiencing stagnation may indicate the need to shift energy and let go. Lack of movement may also convey getting ahead of an intention—it's time to back up and begin again. Or maybe the energy is just moving slowly because of larger collective issues, offering a pause for replenishment. Determining how to respond to potential blocks is an art unto itself. Practice will help you find your way.

Jade has been following an intention to thrive on multiple levels for about eight months. After three years of health challenges, Jade chose her intention, thrive, to help her remain physically vibrant, develop financially sustainable work, and create a work-life balance that included focusing on her photography. For Jade, the root of thriving meant trusting and valuing herself enough to generate her own life.

At first, even though Jade realized that thriving involved moving out of her San Francisco apartment, she was immobilized by fear. She spent months literally packing and unpacking until she learned to hold fear differently inside herself. Shift happened when she found a summer photography internship in St. Louis. The slower Midwest pace would give Jade time to consider next steps for generating work while pursuing her art. When an attractive, affordable sublet quickly appeared in St. Louis, Jade felt she was heading in a good direction. On her way to St. Louis, Jade visited New Mexico and had a special moment with her grandmother, who said, "Jade, you're a bright, beautiful, talented girl, and you can do anything. Take care of yourself." Jade marveled at how life was unfolding.

Life took a challenging turn when Jade arrived in St. Louis to discover a disappointing apartment and a boss reneging on his financial agreement. This lack of financial integrity made Jade begin to question her commitment to the internship. The same day, Jade received a short-term job offer in San Francisco that paid well, including air-fare home. Jade took the job, noticing she was being led back to the Bay Area.

With Jade's return to San Francisco, the pace of life intensified. Fully aware of her intent to thrive, she searched her soul regarding whether to continue the St. Louis internship after the San Francisco job finished. And when her grandmother suddenly died, Jade felt grateful that accepting the internship had made it possible to see her grandmother one last time.

She began seeing the challenges with her boss as a chance to hold boundaries with compassion. As Jade contemplated her contribution to recent jobs, she realized she was valuing herself more. When we spoke, Jade said, "I'm ready for love in my life in a new way." Jade was unclear about where she'd end up living, but she was "trusting and following the energy to thrive."

A few days before she was supposed to return to St. Louis, Jade was lunching in downtown San Francisco when a friend called asking, "Where are you now? I really need your help with a job. Can you meet me?" She was one block away. An hour later, Jade was offered a full-time, salaried job plus moving costs starting in two weeks. After years of contract work, the salaried position represented financial sustainability. Jade accepted the job and traveled back to St. Louis to tie up loose ends. While there, she met a new male friend for a goodbye coffee that ended a day later with a kiss, leaving Jade feeling "changed." Today, just after a few weeks back in San Francisco, Jade recognizes the challenge of balancing both her new West Coast job and her new Midwest guy. But with growing trust, Jade continues to fuel and follow her intention to thrive.

Jade's story reveals how action and synchronicity connect to provide crucial support for forward movement. A job across the country facilitates a final family reunion. A phone call arrives to answer a financial need and also to direct you home. After coming back to your city, a meeting one block away provides a moment of completion to actualize a new reality. And just when you think you're fully living your dream, a casual date stretches your capacity to hold more. Throughout, following your intention becomes a wild, zigzagging trail where each outer step reflects an inward journey on an ultimate path of becoming whole.

Holding and Balancing Expansion without Falling Apart

And now because I've promised to be honest with you, here's some news that sucks. An intention not only helps crystallize wholeness, but it also acts as a red flag so all your unresolved personal material—your fear, hope, and pain—knows just where to enter your life. Jyoti has often said that if you decide to become more peaceful, all those people who drive you crazy are suddenly going to knock on your door. Embodying peace means navigating war. Darlene told me, "We say once you put your intention out there, it's going to come and challenge you somewhere between seven and fifty times." Seven to fifty times!

This annoys me. I mean, here we are doing our best to show up for all this personal excavation; can't we consciousness workers get a break? But that's not the way awareness seems to develop. Holding distinct parts of our lives together creates friction, and we need this friction to learn. In the above, Jade's new job and boyfriend being in two different places will challenge her. Other examples include a devoted but financially struggling artist or a parent who longs to be home but must travel for work. As much as we'd like someone to wave a magic wand to cure our lives, really, we are our own magic wands.

When you recognize how friction grows capacity, challenges become opportunities for growth. They test your ability to maintain consciousness by not collapsing back into dysfunctional patterns of conflict. Darlene explained that the ways you avoid falling back into old patterns and overcome challenges make you who you are. The story of your life becomes a personal myth that can carry you through adversity. When you hold an intention while negotiating tests in daily life, you grow yourself as a magic wand.

As I've mentioned, navigating energy is an experiential practice. The normal level of attachment that comes with a heartfelt intention intensifies stretching beyond what your mind believes you can hold. And the truth is, it's usually a lot. Not collapsing into core patterns during these stretching moments requires help. So, when life is stretching you in challenging ways, how can you hold everything without falling apart?

At these times, moving underneath your individual story and working with the energy of your experience becomes essential. Here, Jennifer's question from the previous chapter about energy speaks volumes. "You've been with this pattern for about fifteen years. What else would you like to do with it?" In these moments of unimaginable stretching, I get really spiritual. I lean into what sustains me, whether it's grounding deep into the earth, dancing to shift energy, or calling upon wise beloveds. I connect with a source bigger than myself because then I don't feel so alone in my holding. I pray, "Please help me hold all this." I watch for synchronicity. I remember my sense of humor. I appreciate a good cup of coffee. I call upon resilience. I question all my attachments. I cry, laugh, belch, sing, shake, and shout to let go. I dig deep to cultivate meaning. Most importantly, I take one step at a time while remembering my intention. As my ego moves aside, I can get behind a challenging energy and navigate it by following my intention.

As always, this isn't about following my way but discovering your own. I encourage you to sit with what supports you to stay awake during uncomfortable times. What helps you move and shift energy? How do you take a deep in-breath between contractions of cultivating your own wholeness? And who or what comes to hold your hand?

My walking prayer is that the eight guides offer some support in holding whatever challenges your life presents. While an intention may wave a red flag, it can also offer a grounding force. When fear shouts in your ear or a core wound nips at your feet, an intention helps you locate yourself in a conversation with the unknown. Arising out of deep intuition, your intention is something to lean into so you can stand strong, hold the faith, and keep on walking, one step at a time. An intention holds the paradox of potential steady, helping you cultivate balance and the capacity to greet the future when it arrives.

EXERCISE: How are you cultivating balance to hold the possibilities your intention is generating? Remember the whole enchilada.

As you become more adept at moving underneath a story to shift energy, the rate of synchronicity increases in your life. Opportunities arrive and you now face the challenge of holding them all. At this point, learning how to balance all the possibilities becomes key. Here, remembering your intention offers pivotal support. In the midst of seesawing among potential choices, intention is a grounding root. Intention also sits at the tip of your arrow to guide alignment as your choices turn into action. From the root to the tip, intention facilitates balance.

Balance also grows from within. The more you hold fears to follow energy, sit with something to develop meaning, and relax into uncomfortable stretching, the more you develop balance on the inside. It's a bit like the chicken and the egg. Holding more teaches you how to find balance. As you practice balancing, you can hold more. Consider a juggler who starts off tossing a few balls together but over time can manage many spinning balls at once. Practicing balance is good preparation for becoming a master life juggler. And what helps you juggle a full life? By anchoring you in the present moment, intention teaches you to hold and balance all aspects of life.

PRACTICE: DANCING THROUGH CHALLENGE

Go somewhere you have access to music and there's room to move your body. Create sacred space. Ideally, you would play some music that is slower and then faster and slower again. Visit *www.dancing-tree.com/ book* for a sample playlist. Turn on the slower music. As you stretch, contemplate one thing in your life that's weighing on you—a feeling, decision, or relationship. Notice where this energy lives in your body.

When you feel ready, turn on the faster music. Remember your intention. Bring your attention to the part of your body holding the challenging energy. As you dance, ask your intention to help you interact with this energy. Explore what it needs, remembering your tools for shifting energy, especially choice and gentleness. Dance with this energy until you feel lighter inside.

Next, put on a slower song and gently transition into stretching. Notice how your body feels. Receive any images, feelings, words, and sensations. Remember your intention again and allow it to inform your experience. When you're finished, close your circle with gratitude.

As you move through daily life, study any changes regarding the challenging feeling, decision, or relationship. Ask your intention to help you grow balance in holding this challenge. Notice any synchronicities. If you're stuck, repeat this practice to shift more energy. With particularly challenging situations, remember to seek wise help.

More Birth Days

Life has been full with my intention for the New Year arriving during a Rhythm & Motion dance class in January. There were many *shoulds* vying for attention, but in the middle of dancing, when I felt the tingling sensation of birth appear, love melted my heart into a big yes. As I was shimmying, I marveled at the twists and turns of my relationship with birth. In recent years, my focus has shifted from supporting conscious pregnancy and childbirth to helping people birth consciousness in many ways. But then a couple months ago, childbirth made a grand re-entrance to anoint me as Nicole's accidental doula. I also attended a second birth. Just over a month later, I was once again officially on call for a birth, my youngest brother's first child. As I stretched, I recognized birth as my root intention. Beyond any form, the essence of birth permeated my life. With joy and gratitude, I felt my intention click into place as I agreed to follow birth's lead throughout the year.

Of course, the Universe began testing my intention the very next day, asking me to follow yet another kind of birth—the expansion of women's Sacred Dance. Jill Pettegrew and I hold a monthly women's Sacred Dance group in San Francisco. In the middle of the year, the door opens for women to leave and join the group. Jill and I had just learned that no one planned to exit our current circle, which meant we would need to turn away the women waiting to enter. We just couldn't accommodate more women in our current space. Realizing several group members were from the East Bay, Jill and I had been sitting with the possibility of a second circle on the other side of the bridge for a while. When someone casually told Jill, "I'd join women's Sacred Dance if you had an East Bay group," we took note.

I decided to do some research on a dance space in the East Bay. Within ten minutes, I found something and emailed Jill, who wrote back immediately, saying, "This is the place I saw and liked, but it wasn't available then!" At that moment, no kidding, another inquiry about Sacred Dance arrived. Well, okay then, message received. We decided to bring this option to our current circle of women the next night. Holding this choice alongside the potential that my sister-in-law could call me away from Sacred Dance and into the birth room any minute was not comfortable. I kept asking birth to help me meet all my commitments.

Thankfully, birth didn't call and I sat at Sacred Dance in awe as women shared what dancing and connecting meant in their lives. As we went around the circle, individual teachings arrived that nurtured the seed of expansion. When it was my turn to reveal the choice we faced, the outpouring of support was immediate. Someone said, "Of course, do it! We want other women to experience Sacred Dance." The East Bay women would miss San Francisco but loved the idea of meeting closer to home. Jill and I proposed an *And* solution to offer a few public Sacred Dances per year so everyone could still connect. Our dance that night contained moments my soul will carry forever.

Three days later, after twenty-four hours of labor, my sister-in-law Bibi gave birth to a beautiful, alert, eight-pound, five-ounce baby boy, Dashiell. My mother was part of the birth team and got my attention when she remarked, "What's amazing to me is how Bibi's intention was so present." Mom knew where I was with book writing.

"There were so many moments when we were hanging on the edge of a precipice and things could have gone any way," my mom recalled. There had been constant misinformation about how Bibi's labor was progressing. "I mean, when Bibi found out she wasn't eight centimeters but four or five, she just moved on. When things happened that she didn't want, she held in there, completely present and making decisions all the way through. My god, she pushed for four hours. Bibi was resilience personified."

A week before going into labor, Bibi had told me she was considering borrowing Lynn's birth intention "to trust no matter what." Shortly after Dashiell was born, I checked with Bibi to see if she really had held a conscious intention during his birth. She said, "My intention was to remember and cherish every moment, no matter how difficult. In other words, my intention was to be present. To show up and remain aware and use that awareness to gain strength and fortitude in order to work through the labor, the delivery, the pain, and to fully experience joy."

I asked if this intention helped her during birth. She replied, "Yes, actually it did. I felt that my birthing team really helped by responding to my requests and my moods and paying attention to how these evolved and changed. But I did remind myself of my intention throughout the process, even though I didn't tell anyone. It really helped me."

Bibi's response delighted me. I can see how her commitment to awareness cultivated the strength for her to move through pain and experience joy. In fact, I witnessed these points converge as Bibi welcomed her son in the world.

It began during pushing. An athletic woman, Bibi was in her element there, often half smiling while resting between contractions. When the doctor arrived and told Bibi she'd been pushing for three hours, Bibi said it felt like thirty minutes. Because normally a doctor arrives just before the baby's delivery, I assumed she was there to move things along.

Instead, our doctor held back and offered encouragement for another hour. By then, we knew the baby was not in an ideal position, and I could tell he was having difficulty coming forward. As we moved past four hours of pushing, the doctor gently told Bibi that while the baby's heart rate had been strong, it was getting time. She wanted to use a vacuum, a small suction on the baby's head. My brother encouraged Bibi to agree. Bibi smiled at the doctor and softly said, "I have some more pushes in me." In unspoken alignment, everyone let the idea settle. Where the baby's heart rate had been consistent all day, I could see him now dipping after a contraction.

At the next resting point, Bibi's best friend and soul sister, Yvonne, leaned close and urged, "Bibi, tell the doctor what you're afraid of, honey."

Bibi burst out, "I'm afraid the vacuum is going to crush the baby's skull!"

The doctor said, "The suction will not crush your baby's skull. I've never had that happen before. See how small it is?" She held up a suction cup.

At this point, I approached. "Bibi, honey, remember that day over breakfast when you said that you wanted to trust no matter what?" She nodded. "Bibi, this doctor has been with us for an hour. That's very rare. No one has pushed interventions. Nothing about this birth has been hasty. You can trust this doctor." My brother touched Bibi's arm and spoke quietly. Then Bibi agreed. Several minutes later, Bibi birthed Dashiell. As my brother and mother followed Dashiell to be checked, Yvonne and Bibi burst into tears and held each other tight.

Bibi started to bleed a lot, and the doctor worked fast. Our nurse rushed in and out of the room, nudging the pediatrician until my brother placed Dashiell on Bibi's chest. Dashiell was alert with his eyes open wide. We all cried and took pictures. When Dashiell fussed for a moment, Bibi instinctively soothed him in Spanish, her native tongue. He quieted right away, clearly recognizing his mama's voice. Then time moved forward, my brother left to get the grandparents, and the doctor stitched. After a bit, the doctor asked where Bibi was from. "Cuba." Bibi answered. The doctor said, "We're from Uruguay."

As the energy of birth settled, Bibi told the doctor, "Don't worry, I'm a bleeder. I hemorrhaged after my second miscarriage." The doctor and nurse glanced at each other.

I said, "Bibi's gone through a lot to become a mother. Two and a half years, right, Bibi?" She nodded while staring deep into her son's eyes.

Then the doctor and Bibi began exchanging personal geography. At some point, Bibi said, "I don't know. My mother died when I was seven."

As gently as when she suggested the vacuum, the doctor said, "And what did she die of?"

Bibi answered, "Cancer. She had brain cancer. Today's the day she died."

The air moistened with poignancy. The wise nurse said, "It's almost like you just got this day back, huh?"

Bibi said, "Yeah. I'm really happy Dashiell was born today." And when the grandparents entered to welcome Dashiell, as if in answer, foggy San Francisco gifted everyone with a clear morning day.

EXERCISE: Remember a moment in your life when different points converged to create a new beginning. Notice if an intention was present to help lead the way.

The Root and the Tip of Embodying Intention

An hour ago, I received an email from Shira. Because she has rectal cancer, Shira has spent the last eight months with an ileostomy pouch after most of her rectum was removed. Alongside mothering two children under the age of four, she's been balancing chemotherapy with alternative healthcare while crap has literally hung out of her body. Tomorrow, Shira's next phase of healing begins with a surgery to close her intestine. Her email asked for support by holding an image of her wrapped in a healing pink blanket of love during the surgery.

Balancing so much has stretched Shira in every way imaginable. "I'm beginning to understand that, for me, cancer is a spiritual practice," she said. "It has asked me to look at all aspects of my life and to clear, forgive, love, renew, and heal on every level." With her intention to hold cancer as a healing journey, Shira embodies the root and the tip of her life. She is a walking prayer. And that's where I see the root and the tip of intention meeting: inside each person as a meaningful relationship that emanates out into daily life. What Shira learns in relationship with healing her cancer develops meaning. Regardless of outcome, Shira embodying her intention shines a healing light that blesses everyone she touches.

Intention guides you through the depths of awakening consciousness by helping you remember yourself from the root through the tip. Intention also integrates the practical and spiritual by asking you to walk your talk through committed action. Backward and forward, inside and outside, embodying the root and the tip of your intention teaches balance as you embark on a journey of wholeness. While you travel step by step, friction builds between fueling an intention from behind with wholehearted commitment—I believe, I believe, I believe in fairies—and resisting the urge to jump ahead with a death grip of attachment. Through this dance of navigating energy, stretching through discomfort grows the capacity to receive your own expansion as a living prayer. At some point, the energy ripens so that the tension feels palpable. Darlene explained, "And that's where the unknown comes in. When we hold the points of paradox so there's space for a third point that we didn't know about to emerge. Then we're allowing our unknowing to unfold." This is that moment of transition in birth when a woman at the doorway of initiation lets go to make way for life. And deep inside the unknown of unfolding life is where surrender lives.

INTENTION GUIDELINES, YOUR INTEGRATIVE QUESTIONS

- What are some gentle ways to remember your book intention?

- How can you practice fierce love for yourself? What choice does your intention represent?

- How are you calling upon your intention to help you navigate pivotal moments?

- How might your book intention relate to a root intention?

- Open focus: what if an orgasm is a metaphor for how to navigate life?

- What steps have you been taking to fuel your intention with action? What's the first step?

- How are synchronistic events expanding your conversation with intention?

- What new possibilities are you experiencing right now? What practices help you stretch so you can learn to hold more?

- How are you embodying the root and the tip of your intention within and throughout your life?

Turning Dead Ends into Doorways

10

Surrender: Accepting Death to Cultivate Life

During this book journey, there's been one teacher emitting flashes of scorching fire from a distance: surrender. I maintained a focus on writing while silently holding the heat until about a month ago when I confided to my mom, "Truthfully, with the way these teachers have been entering my life as I've been writing this book, I'm scared. I mean, really, Mom? Ultimately, surrender is a kind of death. I'm just hoping everyone stays intact."

Mom breathed out and said, "Oh, baby, I get it. But be here now, right, honey?"

I answered, "Yes, Mom. With eyes wide open. The fear is helping me notice the heat. That's all."

And so as I've approached this chapter on surrender, I've been aware of this aching hot fear. A few days ago on the threshold of writing about surrender, I felt another surge. I emailed two friends to call upon their love power. I grounded myself into the earth. I began conversing with surrender, birth, Sacred Dance, and Maitri Breathwork, asking all the healing forces in my life for support. I reminded myself that fear has greeted me as I entered each of these chapter teachers. When I felt the waves of fear begin to flow through me uninterrupted, I relaxed.

Shortly thereafter, I received an email announcing the death of a friend's mother. This friend and my brother have traveled through life—elementary school, high school, marriage, and children—remaining close. A natural affinity plus the boys' wild teenage antics bonded our parents together. This loss hurt.

Through the sadness, I contemplated the powerful force of surrender. I posted a Facebook update: "Staci approaches surrender, the final teacher in her book, with humility. May I be a clear conduit and may this big mama school me with compassionate gentleness." Within a minute, an email arrived from my mother. One of my closest adopted aunts—I call her my tante—was with her mother as she died the night before. My tante was sad but nothing was left unsaid, so she had no regrets. My mother wrote, "It was a good ending."

While a part of me wants to stash my beloveds somewhere safe, mostly I'm aware of the big message of the last two days: surrender is intimately related to death. And death is painful. Death is an ending. Our friends will never experience their mothers' tangible presence again. There's no way around this finality. Nothing will ever be the same.

With death comes change in ways we don't want and can't control. Death leads to the center of the unknown, stripping us bare of any illusions of safety. But rather than recognizing death as a natural part of existence, our culture tries to control death. Issues like abortion and euthanasia magnify how death can become a battle ground for establishing control. Maggi said, "Death is that ultimate expansion of consciousness out of physical form. We're terrified of it, so we make death wrong." Besides control, we escape the grief and loss that comes with death through living in denial. We keep death at bay by idealizing youth and beauty. Ultimately, our culture tries to cage death by demonizing it inside an either/or view of reality.

Turning death into a demon only intensifies our fear. We've learned how suppressing fear into the basement of our lives fills our core foundation with unconscious beliefs, decisions, and relationships. How might our unconscious fear of death permeate daily life?

Jyoti said, "Death's got us tied in knots. It's got us living in fear. It's got our lives. We're imprisoned by this fear rather than embracing life—the beginnings and ends of life as well as the middle of life. We never live life then. We protect ourselves and defend ourselves from it, but we don't embrace it." Besides the actual passing of a loved one, the closest most of us come to facing death is when we feel threatened with some kind of loss. Our unconscious fear of death enters everyday life cloaked inside our fear of loss, endings, and change.

EXERCISE: How might your intention involve facing death, loss, or change of some kind? Perhaps you're feeling stuck and don't want to end a job or relationship. Maybe accepting the reality that life just hasn't worked out as you hoped feels like too much to bear. Contemplate your intention and be honest about whatever loss you're trying to avoid or control.

We've seen how fear of loss and change can constrict choice and thus dictate life. A woman stays in an unhealthy marriage to avoid a perceived unhappy ending. A man hates his job but a fear of failure stifles his ability to leave. But here in the *And* world we're developing together, we don't relegate fear of anything to the basement of our lives. Instead, we shine a light of awareness on fear to help us awaken and grow tools for navigating challenge. And so, because I believe there is a correlation between the amount of fear that greets us on any given threshold with the depth of healing on the other side, a conscious relationship with death could be our greatest teacher of all.

Fostering a conscious relationship with surrender means experiencing all sides of death. You may be familiar with the five stages of grief: denial, anger, bargaining, depression, and acceptance popularized by late psychiatrist Elisabeth Kübler-Ross. Maggi has always added another stage that comes through processing grief: transformation. Birth connects with death, and surrender is the key to holding both.

PRACTICE: GROUND YOURSELF

Because surrender can be particularly strong, please take a moment and ground yourself. Become a tree. Go for a run. Breathe deep into your heart until you feel balanced inside. Listen to music. Call upon helping forces in your life. And remember to fuel and follow your intention one step at a time.

From Giving Up to Letting Go

Dating back to Roman times, surrender has often been depicted as a white flag waving in defeat. In a world where societies competed to survive, losing a battle threatened existence. "In the old days, if you surrendered your country, you surrendered your life. They were met with abuse, those surrenders," said Jyoti. Surrender meant giving up power and losing control.

In many ways, we're still living in a brutal world where we fight to the death over limited resources and surrender can mean annihilation. We only need look at the past ten years of war in the Middle East and Africa for confirmation. At the same time, there are other places around the world, usually more Western or developed countries, where surrender is evolving. Perhaps air travel, the Internet, and global financial markets have intensified interdependence so that devising mutual benefits feels more secure than a winner-takes-all gamble. Maybe as the standard of living has increased for a sector of people, the high stakes surrounding surrender no longer apply. Or maybe by connecting more across different cultures, we've realized a kill-or-be-killed mentality will destroy the very diversity we all need to flourish.

However we've arrived at this new awareness, many people no longer equate surrender with literal death. This eases the fear around surrender. And what happens when we loosen our grip of control around a fear or belief? There's room to grow meaning. Surrender can evolve into a philosophical and even spiritual exploration. Jyoti said, "We're starting to see what it takes to surrender our own ideas in order to embrace more ideas coming from different directions. So we can see the false things and let them go." In an *And* world, neither surrender nor death is wrong. Surrender no longer represents only a battle for survival. In fact, as death's representative, surrender doesn't have to mean giving up at all. This creates room to hold death differently. Surrender can become a choice to let go.

And yet, shifting to an *And* perspective regarding surrender doesn't eradicate fear. At first, choosing to let go can feel frightening. The fear of death is directly linked with the instinct to survive. Here, our relationship with fear as a teacher reminds us that this isn't about killing the fear of death or the urge to survive. I don't believe it's possible or wise to try eliminating these normal healthy instincts. Instead, I encourage you to notice what scares you about letting go without allowing fear to take the driver's seat in your experience. Your intuition can help you sort through thoughts and feelings regarding your fear of letting go to develop wisdom. Sound familiar?

Besides being a physical loss of life, death also contains the energy of change. We've seen how a physical birth can mirror changing consciousness. Birth holds the beginning point of transformation as a form of expansion. Death does the same thing from a different direction, which means that death holds the end point of transformation—the moment of completion.

Here, the teachings from earth-based and women's spirituality help me question some assumptions. What if life isn't a linear process that begins at birth and ends with death? What if instead life moves in a continuous spiral that includes beginning, middle, end, and beginning again, just at another layer of existence? What if birth isn't first at all? What if death sometimes precedes a new life emerging? If a woman doesn't shed her skin through menstruation, she can't grow a baby inside. In gardening, pruning dead leaves is necessary for plants to thrive. In fact, gardeners call compost black gold, as dead organic material produces an especially vibrant garden; rotting greens helps turn a seed into a vegetable.

The earth and a woman's body each cycle through death to generate new life. What if developing consciousness mirrors the natural world? To become whole means we need to consciously remember all our parts. Perhaps we become stuck or immobilized because we haven't developed a conscious relationship with death as a part of life. How can we move forward if we don't know how to let go? We've forgotten to compost the wisdom that lives inside death. Practicing surrender can teach us how to hold death so we can cultivate life in a different way.

EXERCISE: Contemplate a time when you held on to something (a relationship, perhaps) with a death grip to keep it alive. Remember when you chose to let go of something that was dying. How did each situation work out?

Surrender: A Big Mama Practice of Letting Go

Here's an unfair truth: there's usually a specific area in life—something we're quite attached to—that resists our attempts at control. Health. Relationship. Fertility. Parenting. Career. Money. The harder we push, the more obstacles appear. Whether this is our psyche or the mysterious unknown calling, at some point we bump into a reality that shatters our illusion of control. With nowhere left to go, we realize it's time to change direction. If at this moment we commit to surrender, it's possible to discover a whole new way.

Endings hold so much. An ending means the loss of a specific outcome as well as the fears, hopes, and expectations it carried. A relationship breaking up echoes our fears of being alone. Health challenges change reality and threaten a certain existence. Infertility blocks the growth of a family. A job ending raises fear about our value and ability to survive. By exploring what's around and inside an ending, we enter the central training ground for letting go of our attachments.

The nature of surrender isn't gentle. All eight teachers are formidable, but she's the big mama of them all. She isn't soft or acquiescent. She's a primordial, hip-shaking, thick-legged, in-your-face, resistance-shredding, ass-kicking, fiercely loving kind of mama. She can detect the smallest, most invisible strand of attachment. That's why you can't fake surrender (damn it!). Somehow, this big mama always knows. And while I recognize she's quite a lot (how could a change agent of death not be?), I hope you'll take comfort in the fact that you've already met surrender. Growing a conscious relationship with the unknown to develop meaning includes letting go. During this book, you've been practicing surrender through the first six teachers.

Surrender lives within your relationship with fear, awareness, choice, body, intuition, and energy. With its tendency toward dire predictions of failure and loss, fear can block the ability to let go and follow change. But instead, identifying your own particular cast of scary characters loosens fear's grip on your life so you can begin to explore. From there, cultivating awareness by examining your relationships with others, yourself, and specific life challenges sheds light on what no longer serves you. Identifying toxicity often leads to actively letting go by making a choice to transform. Surrender arrives through initiating changes with a beloved, your career, or a personal belief, including releasing the dreams and expectations these relationships held. Letting go can clear space for expansion. As you embody an *And* world, you learn to hold both the pain and beauty of life to explore how they generate wholeness together.

If fear, awareness, and choice are the bones of a surrender practice; body, intuition, and energy are its flesh. As the ultimate doorway for life and death, body is a central initiator of surrender. Body repeatedly calls people into the unknown through surprise illness or inexplicable physical challenge. Here, embodying your senses through noticing how you perceive—vision, hearing, sensation, or feelings—helps you access intuition. Within the depths of truly letting go of all that you know, your intuition is essential for sorting through energy. On the inside, you merge with the primal force of surrender through the crying, dancing, singing, laughing, coughing, body-shaking process of navigating energy. In daily life, you stay behind the energy by noticing the presence (or absence) of synchronistic events that guide next steps or convey when it's time to shift and let go some more.

As you move through life, your relationship with fear, awareness, choice, body, intuition, and energy helps you practice letting go. At first, the pain of letting go of your attachments hurts badly. But over time with increased practice comes the realization that inside the grief of letting go lives freedom, that taking care of life can include a conscious offering of grief as compost for change. Experiencing your grief seriously shows respect for the preciousness of life. So you can't fake surrender, and really, you don't want to. Because a good death is an ending that can help awaken your life. Practicing surrender teaches you how to shift your relationship with the pain of attachment so you can cultivate your own wholeness. No longer stuck, you become free to practice surrender through wholeness as stepping aside allows something bigger to lead the way.

PRACTICE: SURRENDERING AS A WAY OF LETTING GO

Go to your spiritual area and create sacred space. Since it's always possible to deepen relationship, choose an aspect of your intention that feels stuck. Perhaps you'd like to feel your intention more in your body or maybe life events seem to be at a standstill.

Locate the stuck energy in your body. However you feel called, dance, cry, sing, or journal to experience this stuck energy. Gently peel away any layers to see what lives underneath. As you practice shifting energy, ask your intention to help you let the energy go if feels right.

When you've completed, express gratitude and close your circle. Notice what you learned and continue following your intention in daily life. Pay attention to potential synchronicity.

A Young Man, His Wise Teacher, and a House

During our visit, Jyoti shared a story with me:

A young man has heard far and wide about an amazing old teacher. Because the young man yearns to absorb the wise man's knowledge, he gives up everything. He travels and presents himself to the old teacher, sharing his intentions and offering his services as a carpenter in exchange for learning.

The teacher receives the young man graciously. He says that up from the main house where he teaches classes, along a steep, windy trail to the highest mountaintop, there is a house that needs building. The wood for building would need to be hand carried from the main house up the steep, windy trail. The young man gladly agrees to this exchange. While making many trips carrying the wood back and forth to the mountaintop, he passes a constant stream of students attending classes with the teacher.

After spending several months moving all the wood, the young man begins to build the house. As he hammers and saws, he continues to see students coming to the main house for classes with the old teacher, the kind this young man had hoped to attend. His hammering and sawing takes on an angry tone. The old man doesn't seem to care about all his hard work. The teacher has yet to visit him even once. The young man left his entire life behind to be with this teacher, and so far, he's learned nothing. He bangs harder, but because he is a man of his word, he doesn't quit. The young man keeps building until the house is complete.

When the young man finishes the house, he's so proud that he almost bursts through the teacher's door, not noticing he has interrupted the old man eating. The old man barely acknowledges the young man's presence and does not offer him food. The old man finishes eating, and the young man says, "I completed the house, wouldn't you like to go and see it?" And the old man says, "Yes, I guess we should."

As they walk up the steep, windy trail, the young man is fuming. When they arrive, the old man enters the house and kind of cringes, saying, "Well, I could never live here. There's too much anger in this house." The young man has had it. He demands, "Well what are we going to do?" The old man says, "It's bad in here. There's only one thing you can do. You're going to have to take it apart board by board. There are special ceremonies I can give you to cleanse everything, but you must do it all. Then you'll have to put it all back together. But you cannot let this anger come into this building. It just won't do."

Oh, this is a difficult moment. The young man really wants to leave. But he did promise the old man a house, and he keeps his promises. So he agrees. The old man provides details for ceremonies and everything the young man must do to cleanse the bad thoughts living throughout this house of anger. The young man begins, following the instructions to take the house apart board by board. He sees people still coming and going for lessons at the main house. Sometimes this young man gets angry, and when he does, he stops and takes a walk until he feels peaceful enough to return. Bit by bit, after many, many months, the young man takes apart and rebuilds the house.

This time when the young man approaches the old man, he enters the house a little more humbly. The old man greets him warmly, "I'm so glad to see you! It's been such a long time. You've been working so very hard. Let me feed you." After eating, the old man says, "I just can't wait any more! Let's go see the house." He eagerly walks up the windy trail, and upon entering the house, he claps his hands together. "Now this is a house that can be lived in!" Then he looks at the young man and says, "Go get your things and move in. Because this is your house. I'll be waiting for you, as we have more things to learn down the hill." With that, the young man moved into his new house.

Turning Dead Ends into Doorways

Embracing Surrender with Intention-Filled Arms

What first stands out for me in the story Jyoti shared is the relationship between intention and surrender. The young man initiated a conscious journey of letting go by releasing attachment to his old way of life. He followed his intention to be with the teacher. Day after day, he passed through many tests to fuel his intention with commitment. He spent months moving wood up the hill. He built a house. But along the way, the young man became a little lost. He forgot to hold the paradox of learning from the old teacher alongside building a house. He forgot to embody the root and tip of his intention. He got caught in expectation about what a relationship with the teacher should be. He created an either/or reality and cast himself as a victim. Then the wise teacher presented him with a choice. This is where his intention met surrender.

Jyoti said, "The ego expects, and the self allows. In the first part of the story, the young man was meeting his expectations, and in the second part of the story, he was allowing something else to transform him."

As surrender evolves, there's a difference between letting go and stepping aside to allow. Letting go is a death of expectation regarding a human want. We are wired for attachment, but in the face of change, holding on tightly intensifies pain. As the ego learns how to let go and enter the unknown, it softens. In shifting how we hold pain and loss, we find strength in letting go. Our ego begins to heal and find a new place of balance inside. We learn how to step aside and allow. We learn how to follow.

When Jyoti was younger, she remembers feeling like she had to give up a part of herself to surrender. But as she matured, she began to see it more like "the building of a warrior's heart. I had to learn how to get out of the way in order for something larger than myself to be received." When we can get to this place, where we can embrace and allow, we become less defensive. Trust grows.

Peacefulness arrives. We begin to experience powerful forces not as something threatening to harm us, but as a vehicle for expansion.

Allowing often involves sensing the presence of a larger force. For some people, something larger might feel like a spiritual force or some universal energy. It could also be the higher self or a more cohesive self. Sometimes, bigger forces arrive through a surprising turn of events. These can be wonderful gifts of expansion and painful challenges of adversity. Other times, bigness comes through committing to a particular group ideal or vision. Inside the bigness lives a new sense of meaning. To receive the meaning, we must step aside for the bigness to show us the way.

What does stepping aside and allowing feel like? For me, letting go is a death process. Some dream or idea or relationship is no longer serving me. It's time to change. Letting go can feel painful. But then the pain becomes a medium for release. Often, I recognize the need to let go and allow when I notice my ego is holding on too tight. It can feel like a shredding—of my heart, a belief, or whatever I'm gripping too tightly. The pain cultivates awareness that a shift is in order. Getting in the way actually hurts.

Allowing feels different. I visualize my body as a conduit for a larger force and my little self moves aside so this energy can flow through me unobstructed. Often, I recognize a good surrender in hindsight when I notice that an interaction or situation that would have caused pain no longer hurts. I realize I've successfully stepped aside because I feel better. Flow starts to happen inside and throughout my life.

As an example, when Jill and I first noticed the potential for our women's Sacred Dance to expand to a second group in the East Bay, we resisted. Life was already full enough, including this book being due, so we rejected the possibility. My stomach knotted. My intention seemed to nudge me, reminding me of the commitment to follow Sacred Dance and serve this women's circle. When we reached our group capacity and more women kept coming, we realized it was time to step aside and follow Sacred Dance. To expand, we'd need an

Turning Dead Ends into Doorways

East Bay dance space. Within minutes of researching potential locations, the space appeared and we decided to take the leap. As soon as we agreed, I felt a wave of energy release and my stomach relaxed. Within a few days, the expansion landed clearly with two women's Sacred Dance groups emerging.

Moving from letting go to allowing often involves a conscious choice. In the first part of Jyoti's story, the young man let go by leaving his old life behind and presenting himself to the teacher. While building the house, his anger rose to the surface. When the teacher couldn't accept the angry house, the young man arrived at a choice point.

Jyoti explained, "In the second part of the story, the young man had to find God's will. When he had to make that choice, his will could've said, 'Forget you, old man. I'm done with you. I'm out of here.'" But in deciding to stay and learn how to clear the house of anger, the young man stepped aside to receive. When the unknown comes knocking, it's normal for us to throw tantrums of resistance. To truly receive at this time requires letting go of the need to understand and entering a more humble place. Jyoti said, "And when that happens you're most generally rewarded by the Universe. Not because you *expect* the reward, quite the opposite." The house the young man cleared, both inside and out, became his new home.

EXERCISE: Contemplate your intention as it relates to letting go and stepping aside. What further house cleaning needs to take place at this time? How can you shift this energy?

I encourage you to sit with what places you've been clearing and growing in your life as you've followed your intention through this book. Hopefully, like the young man, you've identified some of those angry or scared parts that need tending so you can choose to step aside when that bigger force comes knocking at your door to help you birth another level of wholeness.

Jyoti spoke about this moment of surrender. "It's like transitioning in childbirth when mothers usually say, 'I'm done. I'm out of here. I do not want to do this anymore.' And if they could walk out of the room, they would go. When we're birthing the higher self, people reach that same level, just like this man in the story. And then we have to surrender our individual will to the bigger will, the higher self. The unknown is very palpable at this moment. Usually I can sense it. I can feel it. My ego wants to get out of there, run the other direction because it feels like, whoa, that's going to be too much." Hokhmah Joyallen and I correlate this to transition in labor when a woman dilates from seven to ten centimeters with the energy of initiation. Surrender is a form of initiation.

"There's this separation that starts to want to pull us away from following the higher self. That tension is what Carl Jung would say happens when you're holding the opposites in the moment. If you can hold that tension, without needing to *do* anything about it, just *hold* it, then all of a sudden this third point of possibility that is chosen by the self and not the ego will present itself.

"And then you'll know where you've got to go. You may not like where that is. You may not want to go there. It's that you want to birth that child. And something's pulling you through now. And you're going to surrender to it, and your will and God's will become one will." At this pivotal moment of holding, remembering to embody the root and tip of your intention provides essential support. Intention helps you remain steady as the developmental process of surrender evolves from giving up to letting go to stepping aside. In this way, dead ends turn into doorways for new aspects of wholeness, or even life itself, to emerge.

PRACTICE: EMBRACING SURRENDER

Go to your spiritual area and create sacred space. Remember your book intention, identifying any distinct aspects you've been holding. Call upon the teacher of surrender to help you embody your intention more fully. Ask

Turning Dead Ends into Doorways

to be shown any beliefs, feelings, or energy that might be getting in the way. If you wish, practice releasing this energy to help you make compost for change.

Next, ask the root essence of your intention to come forward. See what it might wish to show you. Listen for any messages. Feel where it lands inside your body. Explore how you can allow the essence of your intention into your daily life so it can lead the way. Offer up some gratitude for whatever inspiration you receive.

Afterward, journal or contemplate your experience to notice what happened, and then close your circle. Be on the lookout for any fears or strong voices trying to throw a tantrum as you move forward. Also pay attention to any synchronicities arriving to facilitate deeper levels of healing.

A Heartbreaking Lightning Bolt of Surrender through My Kira Girl

Six days into surrender, in the midst of writing about surrender as allowing, a lightning bolt struck the center of my family. My beloved fifteen-year-old daughter, my Kira girl—intelligent, funny, and still kind even in teenagehood—woke up one morning screaming in agony. For the first time in her life, I rushed her to the emergency room. There've been no broken bones or even a fever over 102 degrees for my child. She's never had an ear infection, and she's only taken antibiotics once in her life for strep throat. She rarely stays home from school sick. She's that strong, my girl is.

Because the pain was sharp and direct, the doctor said it was either kidney stones or ovarian torsion. "You don't want it to be the second one," he said. When Alex arrived, we joked about his kidney stone genes, how he had had his first serious bout when I was three months pregnant with Kira more than fifteen years ago. As Alex left to get coffee, Kira was no longer screaming. Instead, my child who has been mostly raised on organic food, who didn't eat sugar the first two years of her life, was being placated by a morphine drip.

Out of nowhere, Kira remarked, "It's weird that this is happening when you're writing about surrender."

I asked, "Do you feel surrender coming in here?"

She said, "You don't like hospitals, and I don't like needles."

I let the comment land without response. Realizing what the pages of surrender already held—especially the conversation with my mother when I voiced my fear about everyone remaining intact—my insides trembled. I grounded deep into the earth. Please God, help us.

When the test showed no signs of kidney stones and instead directed us toward an ultrasound, we gulped. "What's a torsion?" I asked the doctor.

He said, "It's when an organ is so heavy with something that it twists on itself."

Kira asked, "How do you fix it?"

The ER doctor, who had told us he had an eleven-year-old son himself, said gently, "It requires surgery."

Kira voiced her upset: She was afraid to be cut. Why couldn't it just be kidney stones like Papa got? She was scared of anesthesia. What if she woke up in the middle of surgery? As Alex and I received Kira's every fear, on the other side of our thin curtain wall, an old man lay wheezing, attended by his healthy teenage granddaughter.

The ultrasound was brutal. Lying down intensified Kira's pain. She held out as long as possible, but then she stopped the tech to breathe her way back to herself, over and over for ninety minutes. As if she were a laboring woman, Alex and I her midwives, we crooned with her through each breath, holding steady in the face of our daughter's agony.

An obstetrician/gynecologist gave us the results. He wasn't a mean man, just too hard, too honest, too fast for my little girl. He told us that somewhere near Kira's ovary or uterus they'd found a large mass, ten by ten centimeters, and they were scheduling an MRI stat. It was a fibroid either near her uterus or on her left ovary. If it was her ovary, it could mean cancer. Surgery would remove her ovary, maybe affecting fertility, maybe not. He outlined cancer treatment quickly: chemo, radiation.

As my daughter burst into tears, I began snarling at this man. "Hold on. Stop talking. You're upsetting her. We don't have any history of cancer in our family." On the inside, I screamed, "Shut up. Back the fuck off." As I wrapped my arms around my girl, Alex stepped in front of the doctor and got him out of our thinly curtained room. It was the first time Kira cried all day.

The MRI happened fast. Alex made jokes about his potential claustrophobia but entered the room to be with Kira. Then Alex and I took turns investigating second opinions, desperately seeking choice. Kira told us she was getting used to the idea of surgery. She just didn't want cancer. "And will I still be able to have children?"

That evening, as Kira was transferred to a pediatric center in San Francisco and Alex went with her, I went home to gather my daughter's list of items. Her computer, makeup bag, soft fuzzy socks from her Christmas stocking, and beloved Lucky, the soft beige horse stuffed animal she's had since she was eight.

Then Alex called me to tell me things had changed. He'd met with "the tumor doctor." This was no single mass in transit between my daughter's uterus and ovary. Weaving in and out and through, this mass had obliterated my daughter's ovary. Gone. The size of a small football, the tumor had to come out. I sank to the floor and listened to my husband. Surgery tomorrow. Cancer screening. Her one remaining ovary would carry the hopes of my future grandchildren, the future children my daughter learned today that she wanted. I got off the phone and sobbed for the first time.

I called my mother. We rallied. She'd already started researching. It could be a benign fibroid. Losing an ovary would not cut her fertility in half. Her other ovary would carry on. Mom said, "Even if it's cancer, adolescent ovarian cancer is different. This is curable, honey. It has over a 90 percent survival rate." I regrouped.

I arrived at the hospital, up three floors from where my family had welcomed baby Dashiell just two weeks ago. When we appreciated having an extra bed to sleep in that night, a well-meaning attendant remarked, "Oh yes. We always make sure oncology patients get their own room because of the risk of infection." As soon as she left, Kira burst out, "Oncology? Does she think I have cancer?" Alex and I encircled Kira and soothed her.

Later, Alex and I met with the tumor doctor together. We were both clear the mass needed to come out. No time for remembering how every morning my daughter pointed to her lower left side, saying it hurt and she couldn't eat breakfast. No time to explain we thought it was intestinal. That the whole family went on a special diet with supplements months ago to address this. Or that I took her to a regular doctor a month ago. Nobody had found anything. We just didn't know.

That night, with our son Noah at my mother's house, Alex and I held each other tightly on the hospital bed across from Kira. As I took comfort in his arms, his body a continuous home, Alex drifted off. I couldn't sleep. The words started moving through me. I fought them until I heard, "Come. Let us sustain you." And so I got up and found a quiet room for the words and tears to unite through me.

After writing most of the above, I turned to surrender. My intention was to be a conduit for these teachers to come through the page for you, the reader, so you could grow a direct relationship. Daily life was supposed to show me what to write. I never ever agreed to this. Not my daughter. Please God, not my precious baby girl.

The conversation with my mother a month ago haunted me. Was it possible the burning heat I felt around surrender had been my intuition trying to warn me about Kira? No. I was not going to blame myself for not catching this reality before it exploded into our life. The doctor said the tumor had most likely been growing inside Kira for at least six months. Synchronicity has always been a friend to me. I needed to trust that healing was happening. In the trials of my friends around me who are mothers—Shira, Dayna—I recognized that my daughter might not be spared this journey. I created an intention: please help me show up for my daughter's healing no matter what. I committed to trusting, following, and living in the unknown of this experience, one step at a time. In the early morning hours at the hospital I wrote:

Kira will most likely lose her ovary tomorrow. She may have cancer. And I'm here. I'm here. In this moment, I'm deeply calling out for surrender to help me. Please show me how to step out of the way to get behind my daughter's healing. Please be gentle if you can. May all the helping forces in Kira's life, everyone who loves her, come now. Please, we need you. Please help bring the right people, the perfect medicine, to her. Please send excellent, honorable, full-hearted doctors, nurses, health practitioners, friends, family, and beloveds. May the grace that has so often gifted Kira please be with us now. Please be kind to my baby girl. Please be gentle with her. She's such a beautiful soul. May she find the strength she needs to thrive no matter what reality appears. May Kira's healing unfold with grace.

Please help me find the strength the hold the paradox of these intentions. To show up clearly for my little girl. Please help me follow, follow, follow. May my mama's ego who wants to hold her precious baby tight remember to trust. May my wisdom self that is alive allow, so that something bigger can lead the way to generate healing, beyond what I can imagine. May miracles unfold. Show me. I'm here. I'm willing.

On the eve of this next step in my daughter's healing journey, I say thank you to Spirit for being with us in this moment even though I don't understand what's happening. I trust that magic is afoot even though my heart is breaking. And blessed writing, thank you for remembering me, thank you for easing my heart tonight. God bless. Peace. Aho. Amen.

With that, I went back into my daughter's hospital room. I wish I could say I slept. I didn't. But as I listened to my daughter's gentle breath flowing in and out of her body, I felt comforted in the moment.

Shades of Grace

When the energy of surrender landed for this chapter, it came with a pretty clear outline. But the nature of surrender is to let go and allow a bigger energy to lead the way. Clearly, what's happening with Kira is a force that needs recognition. Just so you know, one of the few things that tickles my teenage daughter right now is being in this book. I'd give anything to have it be otherwise. Anything.

It's been eleven days since Kira entered the hospital. A terrifying, heart-breaking ride of grief. Kira had surgery. The compassionate, intelligent surgeon did everything he could, but in the end, Kira's ovary needed to come out. Kira could not pronounce the surgeon's name and referred to him as Dr. Hiroshima. The image felt accurate. We've learned that when an ovary is removed, the remaining one works harder and so fertility isn't decreased in half. When the surgeon presented the range of possibilities regarding the tumor, we decided to sit in the unknown about pathology and to focus on Kira's recovery from surgery.

The first few days were a rough ride with Kira spiking a tempera-ture and responding poorly to medication. It seems that my fifteen-year-old doesn't like how narcotics make her feel. She prefers to be present and aware in her body. That's one blessing. Another has been Alex. To see Kira drawing such strength from her papa, turning to him in raw moments in complete trust that he'll meet her there, which he does with every fiber of his being, shows the depth of his fatherhood and humanity. Our twelve-year-old son, Noah, has been the essence of support, changing his Facebook profile picture to one of him and Kira in solidarity and holding his sister's confidences with complete love. When the four of us are together, there's a new ten-derness present, and I can see our teenage children appreciating the preciousness of our family in a new way. Learning how to be in the moment without taking anything for granted, now that's a blessing.

Four days after Kira's surgery, we learned the tumor was cancerous. It's not the adult ovarian kind of cancer but something called dysgerminoma. The doctors say if you have to have ovarian cancer, it's "the best kind." Unfortunately, the tumor broke inside Kira, so she will need chemotherapy. This means she'll be stepping out of high school for the next several months. Our lives are changing in an unimaginable way.

After we found out Kira had cancer, the doctors needed to run some extra tests. During one moment when Kira was getting a bone scan, the technicians started taking extra pictures. Until we met with the doctors for a final diagnosis eighteen hours later, Alex and I sat with the terror that the cancer might be in her bones. Anxiety landed in the center of my heart. When we learned that her bones were fine, that she would mostly likely "just" need three rounds of chemotherapy lasting several months, we were honestly relieved. Given the broken tumor, this is what grace looks like in the realm of cancer.

I keep flashing on an exchange I had with Jyoti. After telling me the story about the young man and the wise teacher, she said, "So I think along the trail with your intention, you must cultivate right attitude."

I said, "Humility."

Jyoti's voice softened into a singsong. "Humility is the key to heaven, they say. I found that to be so. And when I think that I'm quite humble is when I will discover another part of my ego that needs a little more attention. And we have many opportunities for this teacher, humility. Many opportunities. It's all humility, surrender, intention. The rest is all cleaning house. Those were some of the stakes that kept my house from blowing down when the Gods blew hard."

I said, "Humility and intention and surrender?"

Jyoti answered, "Yes. Yes. Because the more you know, the less you know, I came to know. And all the universal teachers said to me, 'Go into any given situation with no need for outcome. Then you will receive healing.' But you must go into life that way. With no expectation, no need for outcome. And then you will follow life, you will approach life, you will live life, in a very, very different way."

I've been living into the wisdom of facing cancer with no need for outcome. In all honesty, it's a point of tension to hold. The mother in me wants to kill this cancer for inhabiting my daughter's body, spirit, life. But rather than hold cancer as a battle, I've decided to treat cancer as a teacher I'm growing a relationship with. Cancer is not a welcome visitor in our lives, but I cannot deny its presence. As her mother, I need to learn how to support Kira in navigating around and through this territory. I'll be watching for the healing gifts this cancer teacher will bring to our doorstep. I will also be studying how to help this cancer leave our lives as safely as possible.

EXERCISE: When life has broken you open, what blessings arrived to facilitate healing?

Standing with Surrender

I've written this book with two types of people in my heart: those who can consciously choose to grow a relationship with the unknown and those who are thrust unwillingly into the unknown through challenging life circumstances. Aside from having a legally blind mother, I was the former. Now I am the latter as well. I'm gratified to discover how, especially when the stakes are high, these teachers I've been writing about offer substantial and meaningful support. A relationship with fear, awareness, choice, body, intuition, energy, intention, and surrender is holding me afloat alongside beloveds in my life right now.

The fear regarding the potential danger and side effects of chemotherapy are already motivating Alex and me to cultivate awareness. We consistently seek to discover choice. Body is not only leading Kira's initiation, but Alex and I are also each digging deep into our body-based practices—his Aikido and my dancing—to constantly restore balance. We're crying hard together. Alex and I both rely on intuition in our own ways to make decisions. We've also agreed to follow this process step by step. Our intention is to stay behind our daughter's healing energy here. Her empowerment is essential.

And so through body as a doorway of initiation and surrender, Kira has been thrust into the unknown. There's no way in hell Alex and I won't be there right by her side. Already we're not alone. My dear friend Shira, the one who has been navigating rectal cancer for the last ten months, has been forging a pathway for an integrative approach to cancer. This past weekend, she gifted us with precious hours sharing her thoroughly investigated resources. We will not be the last to benefit from Shira's healing journey. May this be a reminder how one person growing consciousness can make a difference.

The day Kira, Alex, and I received an official diagnosis from the oncology doctors, Dayna was at the hospital confirming that Dyllan is now showing *zero* rejection on her new heart. After ten months of being apart, the family was reunited this week to celebrate Dyllan's first birthday at home together.

While at the hospital with Kira, I was keenly aware of how privileged we were. Kira's cancer is painful and tricky, but it is considered curable. We were able to leave the hospital after only six days. We had a private room with an extra bed for comfortable sleeping. As an intelligent, resilient young woman, Kira is able to communicate her needs; as a teenager she does so loudly(!). I draw strength from Shira's and Dayna's perseverance and trust they will make good medicine from their journeys. May we hold and follow Kira with such impeccable love, strength, support, and integrity.

It was Jyoti who helped me see the developmental nature of surrender. She also surprised me with an aspect of surrender I hadn't met before. "As I get older, more crone years now, I see surrender in absolutely every parcel of my life. It's in the breath that I take because of my lungs. It's in watching life in the young and the middle aged around me with everybody's different ideologies and ways of acting. There's such a level of surrender in watching life play itself out instead of thinking I have to participate in that. I witness it differently.

"And every day's a blessing because as you get older, your friends are going, your parents certainly are, and so you're sitting with the other end of life a lot. There's another level of surrender that comes into a primal place that I still don't know the word for yet because I'm just starting into that place of study with surrender. But I do see that it's evolved from giving up something to a place of standing with something."

When worked with consciously, the developmental nature of surrender teaches us about different cycles of death as change. We can shift from giving up to letting go and learning how to step aside to stand with the bigness of something. As a woman in midlife, I'm more at the allowing moment of surrender. But in my imagination, I wonder if Jyoti's "standing with" might feel like a leaning in and even merging with a bigger force that guides and holds us. I don't know; I'm just wondering.

....

EXERCISE: Where are you in relationship with surrender?

....

Birth Holds Surrender

In the past ten months, I've watched people around me experience many kinds of transformation. Health crises involving mothers and babies. Marriages going through changes—some have ended while others are starting over. I've also attended three births of beloveds in my life, two with women over forty who never knew they could become mothers. While I'm clear the energy of birth sits at the root of my life, I never expected to enter the birth room again at all, much less three times in the last four months. Birth has once again surprised me with how it's come to claim me. To feel birth with me so strongly at this moment fuels my faith.

Turning Dead Ends into Doorways

My mom noticed that just as I attended three births during book writing, this book could be my third child. As I've shown up to grow this book, this book has grown me. I never ever would have thought that cultivating another level of relationship with these eight teachers would serve as foundational training for the next step in my life: to help my daughter heal through cancer. I honestly don't know where I'd be without this newfound strength (collapsed on the floor somewhere, perhaps). I am eternally grateful.

Yesterday started off as a hard day with Alex and me telling Noah that his sister has cancer. He was brave and sad. But then both kids spent time with close friends. Noah went disco rollerblading. Kira's friend encouraged her to consider some good things that could come from having cancer: a home tutor so Kira can learn at her own pace (fast), online shopping. That night, I could hear my kids laughing while watching a comedy. What sweet music normal life can offer.

When Kira was twelve, she approached Alex and me asking to paint her room red. Kira had just discovered big-hoop earrings, hip-hop music, and shopping. Her body was reshaping into curves, and pimples were appearing on a monthly basis. She was about to begin middle school. Despite her impending teenagehood, she was a responsible student and a mostly patient older sister. So far, Kira had remained true to her kind three-year-old self who used to name ants Antha while carrying them to safety outside. I recognized Kira's wish for red walls as a sign that she was ready to travel deeper into adolescence. After several rounds of negotiation, we arrived at a family painting project of one burgundy wall surrounded by golden creamy colors.

Today Kira told Alex and me that she's ready to change her bedroom again. This time it isn't about painting the walls. Instead, she'd like to rearrange and reorganize everything. She intends to empty and give away her childhood dresser. Alex took the doors off her closet, and Kira spent the day sorting through clothes. Our girl is cleaning house, and I trust she'll find a way to grow a new home inside.

I entered surrender after committing to the intention of birth for this next year. And so birth has been with me as I've studied death. I keep flashing on the moment of initiation during transition in labor when a woman surrenders to make way for new life to emerge. Birth is a universal doorway, as Jyoti says, that when held consciously can also help us learn how to navigate change in life.

My editor Caroline told me that I might discover more than eight teachers through writing. I've just realized that there's been another guiding force with us all along: birth. In this way, surrender is a change agent of death that helps birth new life. And so I've arrived at a point of integration through this book journey: following an intention initiates a dance between fear and surrender that cultivates awareness through choice, body, intuition, and energy to help birth wholeness.

In a dance between fear and surrender, beyond outcome or a heart's desire and even through unimaginable pain, we can learn to navigate the unknown in life. And then the dance changes. No longer bouncing between fear and surrender, we cultivate a way of life that can carry us through anything. We move from fear through surrender to grow the capacity to heal.

You've experienced your own dance between fear and surrender. My hope and intention is that the points of paradox you've held have helped you develop your unique relationship with the unknown. There are so many ways to embody choice in navigating life. May the healing tools you've grown serve you well. And may traveling from fear through surrender help you realize a path of meaning to birth yourself whole.

SURRENDER GUIDELINES, YOUR INTEGRATIVE QUESTIONS

- What might a conscious relationship with death look like in your life? What fears regarding death, loss, or change are holding you captive?

- How have you been practicing surrender in your relationship with the first six teachers?

- How has your book intention facilitated surrender in your life?

- Overall in your life, where are you in your relationship with surrender as giving up, letting go, allowing, or standing with something?

- What's left to clean in your house? Where do your will and God's will meet (or not)?

Afterword

When Kira was thirteen and Noah was eleven, we visited New York City. As we approached a busy SoHo intersection I said, "Be careful—pedestrians don't automatically have the right of way here." As Noah and I gripped hands and peered hesitantly toward a stampede of honking yellow taxicabs, Kira's shoulders relaxed and she stepped off the curb, taking alert yet assertive strides to calmly negotiate oncoming traffic across the street. More than her New York genes rising to the surface, it was as if Kira's bones recognized the quick, bold vitality of Manhattan as home.

Now Kira's almost sixteen, and it's been six months since Kira was diagnosed with a rare dysgerminoma cancer. Six months that included three surgeries, four rounds of chemotherapy, and over seven weeks of accumulated hospital time before Kira's cancer thankfully went into remission. Going from emergency surgery to the first round of chemotherapy within two weeks felt overwhelming; there was no time to fully implement an integrative approach to satisfy my holistic preferences. Yet, recognizing the energy of my daughter's clear assertive steps in approaching cancer urged me to trust and follow the fast pace of forward movement.

A favorite quote in our household during the four months of intensive chemotherapy came from Winston Churchill who said, "If you're going through hell, keep going." For me, cancer initiated a journey through the underworld. On the one hand, my daughter was the young Greek goddess Persephone, taken into a cancerous hell, losing her innocence alongside her cap of golden brown curls. On the other hand, I didn't feel like Persephone's mother, Demeter, left above ground to scour the earth, creating an eternal winter without food to demand her daughter's return. I was able to travel with my daughter, channeling my grief to help her navigate this relentless underworld.

Throughout this book we've discussed consciously holding points of tension in your life as they interact to create new form. The process of holding while life stretches you open mirrors transition during childbirth as an initiation into surrender. Letting go of feelings, expectations, or relationships and stepping out of the way to make room for a bigger force to appear leads to rebirth. Sometimes different aspects of your life converge into beautiful aha moments of completion while other times painful new realities emerge. You may not always like what arrives, but you don't waver because letting go and stepping aside is how you've demonstrated your willingness to take care of life.

As a healing practitioner who cares deeply, I really want your daily life to reflect the beauty of your blooming heart. I want you to be happy. And yet the spiraling nature of life needs to include every cycle—birth, maturity, decline, and death. Constricted with fear, our culture has split the cycle of life into good and bad parts; we deify young or happy and demonize old or painful. We've been holding on to happiness with a death grip of attachment. So, as much as I want you to be happy, my commitment is to help you reclaim every part of yourself so you can become whole. This includes learning how to consciously let go, allow, and stand with loss, endings, and even death itself as a natural part of change in life. Beyond right or wrong, good or bad, happy or painful lives an *And* world where you can inhabit your fullest self by accepting it all.

In the past few days, I've encountered people committed to an *And* way of life. After several years of struggle, a friend is letting go of her marriage. With two children and expectations about the definition of family, this ending feels like a death. She said, "It's a loss that's also given me something. It's like I'm opening my eyes and finding an adult standing in the room—me." Meanwhile, a year after a client of mine completed grieving his seven-year relationship, he's starting over by moving in with his new love. Shira's healing journey with cancer continues as she combines allopathic and alternative treatment. And baby Dyllan, who is approaching the one-year anniversary of her heart transplant, just completed a biopsy that once again confirmed zero rejection for her new heart, on her mother's birthday.

Because I asked eight teachers to show me what to share through daily life happenings and chronicled my journey here, the converging of points of big mama surrender and Kira being diagnosed with cancer was a lightning bolt through my heart and frankly, this book. I would have preferred to give you a tidier ending. Instead, to remain true, the reality of my daughter's cancer exploded from my life onto the page. While tending to my family these past months, I've been sitting with potential meaning.

I've often revisited the intense heat I felt radiating around the teacher of surrender that I described at the beginning of that chapter. For me, it illustrates how fear and intuition work together to increase awareness. As to whether the blazing fire came from the force of surrender, my daughter's cancer diagnosis, or their convergence, I just don't know. While everything in me wishes we had known to ask for a sonogram, with no significant history in our family and no blood markers for this type of cancer, the possibility of cancer wasn't even a blip on anyone's radar. And so with profound sadness, I'm left at a choice point regarding trust.

Yesterday I met with Jade, the woman whose intention to thrive has led to a new job in San Francisco and love in the Midwest. Jade's life hasn't been easy; her mother died when she was a child, and she spent the last few years recovering from a debilitating digestive condition. Jade told me, "The root of thriving is about trusting whatever teacher is going to show up in my life. Even the teacher of scarcity." I said, "So really, thriving means trusting yourself to be able to navigate what life brings you." Maybe trust isn't a guarantee that life will work out the way you dream. Instead, trust is an opportunity to grow what you need within yourself through each moment.

I don't pretend to understand the presence of cancer in our lives, much less the timing of its appearance. But based on everything I hold as sacred, including how I invited synchronicity to inform this book in real time, I'm choosing to trust what life has been asking me to grow. Kira went to the emergency room the day after I began writing about surrender as stepping aside to follow big energy. If the burning heat of surrender helped me accept the loss of Kira's ovary in order to remove the tumor or showed me how to stand with my daughter in an unfamiliar allopathic world, if my awareness of surrender made me a better mother in any way, I am eternally grateful. Because resisting would only have helped cancer consume my daughter's body further. And in my eyes, surrender and Kira's cancer diagnosis converged to birth a third vital force to follow: my daughter's healing.

Kira is a precious daughter, adored older sister, dear friend, bright student and beloved eldest great-grandchild, grandchild, niece, and cousin on all sides of her family. Everyone in Kira's world has been initiated into body as the ultimate doorway for awakening consciousness. Now that includes you, through how I was guided to write this book.

And so while I'm sorting through grief to find meaning from my daughter's healing journey, I invite you to do so as well. I've shared how my relationship with the eight teachers held me steady in the early days of Kira's diagnosis. I don't believe that recognizing these teachers as a dynamic force for navigating the unknown of daily life created Kira's cancer. At one point, my editor, Caroline, wondered if we should slow publishing to give the book a chance to catch up to my life. Since I edited the first draft of the book while sitting across from my daughter during her second round of chemotherapy, I had been asking myself if I stood by the material in light of what was unfolding. Caroline's question made me realize my life was catching up with the book, not the other way around.

The relationship I forged with the eight teachers through writing the book merged inside my being as a root and compass for weathering Kira's healing crisis. A ten-minute break when I cried, shook, and called upon my great-grandmother Baba from the ethers for strength defused the terror burning in my heart enough to sleep for a while. Women's Sacred Dance cradled my aching mother-self and then snapped me out of potential indulgence, showing me how to move with each moment to remember my power. When I crashed into despair, contact with beloveds helped me find new points of balance. Throughout, as I danced between fear and surrender, I followed my intention by relying upon intuition and body wisdom to notice energy and generate choice. My relationship with the eight teachers was not a mental construct or a privileged afterthought but foundational support that kept me standing amidst the pain so I could navigate cancer and mother my two children in an authentic way.

As I traveled through my daughter's treatment noticing how I was integrating my relationship with the eight teachers, I didn't forget about you. I wrote this book for two kinds of people: one who can take an in-breath of choice before consciously entering the unknown, and another who is thrust forward by challenging life circumstances. It was one thing for me to arrive at this merging based on many years of following and developing Practical Spirituality, but how would this book serve someone with less mileage in consciously navigating the unknown?

The heart of Practical Spirituality does not only live within these pages as an approach and creative practice for consciously navigating energy. Practical Spirituality also rests inside the relationships you grow. What invigorates Practical Spirituality is your heart, your life, and the path of healing you cultivate to birth yourself whole. Within that, because relationship requires effort, we rarely do something well the first few (hundred) times, and because I appreciate gentler healing when possible, I'd prefer that everyone get to take a big in-breath of choice before entering the unknown. Reading usually begins with learning the alphabet and probably happens more easily in a relaxed atmosphere, yes?

And yet, clearly, sometimes the unknown breaks down the door without our permission. In writing this book partially as a love letter to anyone surrounded by a terrifying unknown, I had no idea I would literally end up there myself. I realize it might be difficult to create sacred space in your home and complete each exercise if you're juggling a sick child in the hospital or are yourself experiencing chronic pain. One of the most challenging aspects of going through something shattering is that it isolates you from daily life and makes you feel alone. Even in the company of caring people, the heaviness of holding unimaginable realities can be too much for some people to bear.

In the hospital during the extreme sensitivity of chemotherapy, though my daughter could not tolerate electronics or sudden movement inside her room, she was fine with the quiet turning of a page from a book. If one teacher, one paragraph, one person's story here helps you draw an in-breath, I am grateful. This book and my current life experience urge me to convey that you don't need to be alone inside whatever loss you're facing. You can remember choice to sustain yourself wherever you are. Please know that my heart continues to be with you.

Yesterday, Kira rejoined her tenth-grade class for her first day back in high school. Cancer has moved to the periphery of our lives, but it is not gone. My girl will face regular testing for reoccurrence, but her focus is clear. After reorganizing her bedroom during treatment, Kira hung an oversized tapestry of a tree that stands seven feet tall and five feet wide. On cream cotton, dark roots form a solid trunk of branches gracefully extending far and deep to hold a tree full of buds that will someday blossom. In two weeks, we will celebrate the Bar Mitzvah of our son, Noah, a Jewish rite of passage into adulthood. Instead of a sports theme, Noah has chosen potted plants as centerpieces for each table to be identified with words he's selected: happiness, health, bravery, love, hope, laughter, inspiration, family, and friendship. Next month, I'll experience a different rite of passage when my intention, birth, leads me full circle to reenter the labor room as a professional doula. As I write this, Alex and the kids are upstairs making gluten- and milk-free pancakes for breakfast. Together, my family is fueling our commitment to grow a new normal, cultivating our own tree of life one leaf at a time.

On the inside, I'm left to balance some new unknowns. A part of me remains in the underworld, not lost but gathering a few things. I can be patient with this unknown, but accepting other uncertainty, especially regarding my children, is requiring more practice. After experiencing the fragility of life, I'm raw from stretching deep into the vulnerability of not knowing. The mother in me is greedy for my children's happiness. I want to bank every normal minute so they can amass a wealth of resilience to carry them through whatever reality appears. At the same time, if we become so busy grasping at certainty, we miss the point of connection: to experience the precious gift of life present in each moment.

In the dance between holding and letting go, loosening your grip of attachment is what activates choice and grows your power. Not the kind of power that creates only beautiful realities and keeps pain at a distance. The kind of power that comes from realizing your capacity to dance with whatever life brings you. Power that includes accepting graceful expansion along with agonizing loss while remembering not to hold on too tightly to any of it. After all, life is change. You grow your power through developing relationship with every part of life, every aspect of yourself. Over time, practicing helps you discover your own rhythm of relationship to cultivate a path of meaning. You become whole enough so you can step aside and follow.

Through whatever teachers you invite into your life, or perhaps those that land on your doorstep, I wish you a healing journey. No matter how far or deep you travel in navigating the unknown of yourself and daily life, may you remember that it's never too late to start over, and in fact, you've only just begun. So that as you transform through many cycles of death and birth inside the unknown, your eyes remain open to connect with the trustworthy adult standing strong, open-hearted, and fully present in the room, and that adult is you.

BOOK GUIDELINES, INTEGRATIVE QUESTIONS

- Which fears make up the cast of characters in your life? What fears play both starring and supportive roles?

- How has fear helped you cultivate awareness? How do you tend to notice feelings, beliefs, and energy inside yourself and daily life?

- What choices are you making in your relationships to embody an authentic empowered life? How are the Triangles helping you?

- What ways does your body constantly awaken your consciousness? How are you listening to your body? How are you respecting and celebrating your body as sacred space?

- Which senses help you access intuition? How do you sit with and hold decisions, projects, and relationships to generate wisdom?

- What does staying behind to follow energy feel like to you? How do you shift and transform energy within and throughout your life?

- What have you learned from embodying the root and the tip of your intention for this book? What is your root intention in life?

- How do you recognize when it's time for you to let go of a belief or relationship?

- What parts of your ego needs attention to rebuild your metaphorical home? How are you getting out of the way to follow something bigger in your life? How are you standing with this force of awakening?

- How are you experiencing your world, inside and out, differently? How have you been tested and gifted through relationship with the eight teachers? What points have converged to help you birth a new way of life?

- What are three main ways you navigate the unknown?

- What healing gifts have you grown through a conscious relationship with the unknown?

- How is healing happening right now, this very minute in your life?

Acknowledgments

Just as it takes a village to raise a child, birthing a book cannot happen alone. Thank you to my book midwife, Caroline Pincus, associate publisher at Red Wheel/Weiser Books and Conari Press, for her integrity and keen intelligence. From a chance meeting at the gym to a beautiful book collaboration, really, Caroline, there are no words for how you've touched my life. I'm also grateful to the team at Conari Press for demonstrating commitment to emerging work by publishing first-time authors like me: Thank you Robin Doyle, Susie Pitzen, Jim Warner, and Ali McCart.

To my husband, Alex, thank you for being an honest sounding board, zigzagging across the city to tend to our family many a weekend as I wrote, and for always being willing to hold my hand to help me fall asleep. To my most precious teenagers, Kira and Noah, from cooking dinner or catching a bus home to letting me write about you, I appreciate your support; you are the best ever. Thank you to my three living grandparents Herb Boden, Ethel Rotman, and Ida Theobald for always believing in me. And I wish to thank my parents for a foundation of consciousness that inspired my life: to Mom for exemplifying healing as empowerment every day, to Dad for connecting me with Spirit, and to Punkin for giving me Technicolor love.

I am deeply grateful to the invisible world and all my sacred relationships for guiding this book. I also appreciate those human teachers who have grown my mystical wings with practical feet (in order of appearance): Hilda Charlton, Meenakshi Kramvik, Maggi Quinlan, Jennifer Sugarwoman, Jyoti, Russell Park, and Darlene Hunter. Thank you to kindred travelers for how we've followed healing energy together: Sue Lockyer and Jill Pettegrew for Sacred Dance; Jennifer Sugarwoman, Dayna Wicks, and Margaret Lindsey for Maitri Breathwork; and Hokhmah Joyallen for Birthing Intuition. I'm thankful for the impeccability of the Kayumari community and the Center for Sacred Studies.

In the realm of words, I appreciate Consuelo Faust for embracing my love for dance in Rhythm & Motion Dance Workout Program's newsletter that informed the body chapter here. And I offer everlasting gratitude to author Sage Cohen, my angel mentor, who from blog to book proposal nurtured my writing voice into song.

To those who also sustain me, thank you: Mark Levitan for decades of spiritual connection; Shira Shaiman for fierce love; Mara, David, and Ethan Johnson for treasured family time; Maria Rogers Pasqual for strength in motherhood; Courtney Courtney for joyful singing; and especially my rock, Nicole Davis, for being a constant safe harbor. I also wish to acknowledge my beloved clients, friends, and family who did not hesitate in allowing their intimate experiences onto these pages to help people heal. Finally, dear reader, thank you so much for your time, trust, and courage in traveling with me through the unknown; may what you grow serve you well.

About the Author

Kira Boden-Gologorsky

Staci Boden is a San Francisco-based writer, healing practitioner, and energy worker. Through her company, Dancing-Tree Consulting, Staci works with individuals and groups to help transform decisions, projects, and relationships. She sees private clients as well as leads personal and spiritual development workshops in energy work, sacred dance, breathwork, and guided visualization to help people learn how to navigate life.

As a feisty teenager, Staci didn't buy the you-can-create-your-own reality interpretation of how her legally blind mother should heal her eyes. Instead, she has devoted her life to developing a Practical Spirituality® approach to living with meaning in the face of the unpredictability of life. Practical Spirituality teaches people how to navigate the unknowns in daily life while weaning them from the illusion that we can *control* outcomes.

She holds a Master's degree in Women's Spirituality from the California Institute of Integral Studies and is a certified doula (birthing facilitator).

Visit Staci at *www.dancing-tree.com.*

To Our Readers